10 SUCCESS FACTORS FOR LITERACY INTERVENTION

Praise for *10 Success Factors for Literacy Intervention*

10 Success Factors is the perfect title for this book. Too often, key factors in literacy intervention in a Multitiered System of Support (MTSS) have not been considered or implemented. With an easy, understandable style, Dr. Susan Hall clearly describes 10 factors that, if implemented, will increase the success of literacy intervention. Leaders, coaches, and teachers responsible for student growth in reading will find this a valuable resource for reflecting on their current practices, determining factors that may be missing, and implementing needed success factors to increase their students' reading outcomes.

—Deb Fulton, Former State-Wide Lead for Literacy,
Pennsylvania Training and Technical Assistance Network (PaTTAN)

Dr. Hall has a proven track record of improving the interventions student receive, and with this book she has provided a substantial resource for any school or district not getting the most from their program. The examples, protocols, and templates she provides are doable and are sure to cause real change in how you serve your students. This truly is essential reading for anyone working to move their intervention program and their students to the next level.

—Trey Duke, Coordinator, Federal Programs and RTI,
Rutherford, Tennessee County Schools

We have been implementing the *10 Success Factors for Literacy Intervention* districtwide over the last three years in kindergarten through 3rd grade. We are very excited about the focus our teachers now have for reading intervention, the success they are beginning to see, and the reading skills our students are learning. As a result, our teachers have the opportunity for professional conversations through research-based common language that guides their ongoing decision making about the teaching of reading. This gives us hope that we can make a significant difference in the number of students reading on grade level by the end of 3rd grade.

—Clare Gist, EdD, Superintendent, Tulare City School District
Tulare, California

What a resource! Whether your school is just developing its MTSS process or it's in need of an overhaul, you'll find what you need here. Straightforward and practical, Dr. Hall shows how success for all students is within reach.

—Kim Stuckey MEd, LPC, Dyslexia Consultant

ASCD MEMBER BOOK

Many ASCD members received this book as a
member benefit upon its initial release.

Learn more at: **www.ascd.org/memberbooks**

SUSAN L. HALL

10 SUCCESS FACTORS FOR LITERACY INTERVENTION

Getting Results with MTSS in Elementary Schools

 ascd

2800 Shirlington Rd., Suite 1001 • Arlington, VA 22206 USA
Phone: 800-933-2723 or 703-578-9600 • Fax: 703-575-5400
Website: www.ascd.org • E-mail: member@ascd.org
Author guidelines: www.ascd.org/write

Deborah S. Delisle, *Executive Director;* Stefani Roth, *Publisher;* Genny Ostertag, *Director, Content Acquisitions;* Allison Scott, *Acquisitions Editor;* Julie Houtz, *Director, Book Editing & Production;* Miriam Calderone, *Editor;* Judi Connelly, *Associate Art Director;* Donald Ely, *Senior Graphic Designer;* Cynthia Stock, *Typesetter;* Mike Kalyan, *Director, Production Services;* Shajuan Martin, *E-Publishing Specialist;* Andrea Hoffman, *Senior Production Specialist*

PAPERBACK ISBN: 978-1-4166-2617-6   ASCD product #118015
PDF E-BOOK ISBN: 978-1-4166-2619-0; see Books in Print for other formats.
Quantity discounts are available: e-mail programteam@ascd.org or call 800-933-2723, ext. 5773, or 703-575-5773. For desk copies, go to www.ascd.org/deskcopy.

ASCD Member Book No. FY18-8B (Jul. 2018 PS). Member books mail to Premium (P), Select (S), and Institutional Plus (I+) members on this schedule: Jan, PSI+; Feb, P; Apr, PSI+; May, P; Jul, PSI+; Aug, P; Sep, PSI+; Nov, PSI+; Dec, P. For details, see www.ascd.org/membership and www.ascd.org/memberbooks.

Library of Congress Cataloging-in-Publication Data

Names: Hall, Susan L. (Susan Long), author.
Title: 10 success factors for literacy intervention : getting results with MTSS in elementary schools / Susan L. Hall.
Other titles: Ten success factors for literacy intervention
Description: Alexandria : ASCD, [2018] | Includes bibliographical references and index.
Identifiers: LCCN 2018008398 (print) | LCCN 2018025260 (ebook) | ISBN 9781416626190 (PDF) | ISBN 9781416626176 (pbk.)
Subjects: LCSH: Reading—Remedial teaching. | Reading (Elementary) | Response to intervention (Learning disabled children)
Classification: LCC LB1050.5 (ebook) | LCC LB1050.5 .H257 2018 (print) | DDC 372.43—dc23
LC record available at https://lccn.loc.gov/2018008398

27 26 25 24 23 22   6 7 8 9 10 11 12

To my supportive husband David and
our two children, Brandon and Lauren

10 SUCCESS FACTORS FOR LITERACY INTERVENTION

Getting Results with MTSS in Elementary Schools

Acknowledgments

Writing a book is a family affair because it affects the time I have available to be with my family. This is my eighth book in 18 years; there's no way to estimate the number of hours I've spent writing books. This one was particularly stressful because the manuscript was submitted three days before our son's wedding. This book is dedicated to my husband David and our children, Brandon and Lauren. Thank you for your support while I wrote this book.

I'd also like to acknowledge the consultants and sales executives at 95 Percent Group, whose insights are woven into the ideas shared in these pages.

Finally, this book would not have happened without the amazing administrators and teachers in our company's client schools. Thank you for letting me learn with you.

Introduction

Educators are repeatedly enamored with the latest shiny penny. Over the last 25 years, initiatives have come and gone, shining brightly for a while and becoming the focus of excitement. Then, just as results begin to surface, attention shifts to the next promising initiative. When attention veers off, good ideas disappear—just as schools were starting to figure out how to implement them. Remember open-concept classrooms (classrooms without walls), learning styles, looping, 21st century skills, and brain gym? Educators want to believe that the hot new idea is sure to be the silver-bullet approach to education reform. If any of these initiatives were the answer, why haven't schools seen impressive gains over the long term?

With these observations in mind, why would anyone write a book in 2018 about Response to Intervention (RTI), or Multitiered Systems of Support (MTSS)? Isn't it on the decline? Actually, that's exactly why this book is needed now. Instead of focusing on strengthening MTSS implementation, attention has shifted to the newest thing. Three initiatives that are currently "hot" are personalized learning, flipped classrooms, and 1:1 technology programs that provide all students with laptops, iPads, or smartphones. How could such a fundamental idea as MTSS be treated as a fad that risks replacement by newer initiatives?

MTSS just makes good sense. It's a framework for schools to establish systems to identify struggling readers and to use data to differentiate instruction delivered in small groups, known as "tiers," to address students' identified skill deficits. It should be as fundamental to how elementary schools operate as assigning students grade levels, dividing students into homerooms with an assigned teacher, and organizing the day with a master schedule. A systemic approach to differentiating instruction to meet the needs of all students should be nonnegotiable. It's not a fad, and it shouldn't be pushed aside for something else that draws the staff's attention.

> The reason results have not been consistently strong is that in implementing MTSS, too many schools have left out critical components.

One reason it may be easy to push aside MTSS is that although results have been outstanding in some schools, they have been negligible in too many others. With mixed results, MTSS is now vulnerable to being overtaken by other initiatives. Yet the reason results have not been consistently strong is that in implementing MTSS, too many schools have left out critical components. Author David Kilpatrick (2015) states, "In developing the framework and process of RTI, the highly effective intervention methods that provided such outstanding results were left behind" (p. 14).

Kilpatrick's statement is true. However, it's more than proven instructional methods that have been left out of implementations. The systems and processes at the heart of MTSS have been left behind as well. Many schools think they are implementing MTSS, but their framework lacks some components that are critical to success. Those omissions explain the need for this book.

Why I Wrote This Book

Nearly every week of the school year, about a dozen consultants from my education consulting and professional development company, 95 Percent Group, are working in schools. We help hundreds of schools implement MTSS every year. During workshop presentations and onsite coaching visits, we learn what schools around the United States are doing in literacy under the name of "MTSS" or "RTI." It's not surprising that results are disappointing when so many components that make it work are missing.

Given the varying effectiveness of MTSS, the obvious question is, what are schools that are getting good results doing? When results are unimpressive, what's missing? These questions led to the development of a list of 10 success factors observable in schools that are getting significant gains in student literacy with MTSS. The goal of this book is to illuminate these success factors with the hope that MTSS won't be one of those short-lived shiny pennies that disappears when the next initiative hits the scene. MTSS deserves to stay.

My Personal Story

I'm passionate about teaching teachers how to identify and address the needs of struggling readers. My passion comes from a personal story that started many years ago when my son was in 1st grade. One day he came home from school and asked me the following question: "Mom, why am I in the top math group and the lowest reading group?" I replied, "I don't know, but I'll find out."

That question began our family's journey. His 1st grade teacher could not have been any warmer or more encouraging to all her students, including our son. He went to school eager to learn, and we had done everything parents do to prepare their children to learn to read. We talked to him constantly and read to him every day. He entered school with a robust oral vocabulary, and he knew the alphabet.

> Given the varying effectiveness of MTSS, the obvious question is, what are schools that are getting good results doing? When results are unimpressive, what's missing?

When we first asked our son's teacher why he was in the lowest reading group, she said that boys sometimes develop later than girls and not to worry. At our spring parent-teacher conference, we asked if our son had moved up in reading groups. After she reported that he was still in the lowest reading group, we asked if he should be tested. His teacher said no and explained that she couldn't possibly refer him for testing because he wasn't a year behind yet. In the school's eyes, he hadn't failed yet. But in his eyes, he had already failed. His math abilities led to his placement in the highest group in that subject, but because he couldn't read like the other kids, my son felt he was failing in school. First graders think that the kids who can't read well are dumb.

At this point we took matters into our own hands and paid for a private evaluation. The psychologist told us that our son is dyslexic and so was probably never going to read well. Furthermore, this psychologist told us that it was unlikely our son would ever attend college. For two parents with graduate degrees, can you imagine how that felt? To say that we were panicked would be an understatement. Our son immediately began private tutoring, and my fascination with his struggles led me to return to graduate school, ultimately earning a doctorate in education.

Yet this story is not about our son's dyslexia. With a lot of great advice and a significant financial investment, we forged a path that enabled our son to go to college and graduate school, and he is now a successful architect. If his elementary school had been able to provide the instruction our son needed, we would have advocated for his qualification for special education services. Although it was the impetus, our son's experience with dyslexia has not been the focus of my career. What crystallized my life's mission was actually the contrast between the experiences of our two children in 1st grade. Our daughter, who is two years younger, had a different 1st grade teacher in the same public elementary school outside of Chicago. These two teachers taught reading completely differently. Our daughter's teacher had a deep knowledge of phonics and taught reading very explicitly. Our son's teacher used authentic literature and taught skills incidentally, only as students experienced confusion about words in text. His 1st grade teacher, as loving and caring as she was, had *no* idea how to help our son learn how to read. Our son needed the teacher his sister had, and our daughter would have read well with any teacher. I'm not going to tell you that our son could have learned to read without the multisensory structured language tutoring he had. His situation is different from many students' because he is dyslexic. However, what bothered me was a nagging worry about how U.S. schools were going to ensure that children learn to read well before they leave 3rd grade.

Our family's experience with two 1st grade teachers sparked my grapple with three pesky questions:

- What happens to kids who get off to a slow start in reading?
- Why do elementary teachers know different things about how to teach reading?
- Why doesn't every teacher have the knowledge and toolkit to help every child learn to read?

These questions led to my decision to start 95 Percent Group. Our passion is to inform and support teachers. We believe in teachers. They are good people who are dedicating their lives to improving the lives of their students. Yet they haven't been provided what they need to teach all students to read. Our goal is to provide teachers with the knowledge to identify struggling readers, pinpoint their deficits with assessments, and provide effective intervention to address their needs. No technology to date has been proven effective at teaching children to read without a teacher; teaching reading is a complex process. Schools need informed teachers who possess a deep knowledge base about the brain processes involved in reading and the best instructional practices that have been supported by reading research. My dream is that every elementary teacher in the United States have a toolkit and a knowledge base to teach every student how to read.

A Note About Terminology

Authors often struggle with how to deal with the "he/she" quandary. Should the entire book always use the masculine *he*, switch between *he* and *she* every other chapter, use *he/she* everywhere, or mix them? In this book *he* and *she* are mixed without any intentional difference. When you read one or the other, just consider them interchangeable.

Another dilemma in writing this book is which term to use: *RTI* or *MTSS*. As noted earlier, *RTI* stands for "Response to Intervention," and *MTSS* stands for "Multitiered Systems of Support." This book will call it MTSS, because that's the term that is currently more common in the United States. Some educators say that MTSS is more comprehensive than RTI because, at a minimum, it typically includes literacy, math, and behavior, and it may also include science and social studies. In some places, RTI includes only academic areas.

Both RTI and MTSS are labels for something that was previously called by other names. The term *RTI* started to gain traction in about 2005, and the use of *MTSS* is more recent. Before that, at least in the area of literacy, it was commonly called "Early Reading Intervention." Although it didn't include everything that's in our current view of RTI or MTSS, Early Reading Intervention had many of the same elements. One difference is that the framework is more structured now. The focus of Early Reading Intervention was on identifying kindergarten and 1st grade students who lack precursor literacy skills with the goal of providing immediate small-group support, because early intervention results in faster progress than providing help in 3rd grade or beyond.

Finally, it is worth mentioning that MTSS in one state doesn't mean the same thing as MTSS in another state, which presents a challenge. Once again, in this book, *MTSS* means Multitiered Systems of Support.

What Is MTSS?

As noted earlier in this Introduction, MTSS is a framework to identify students who are not achieving at benchmark levels and to use data to inform decisions about what supports will help them reach expected performance. An MTSS framework typically includes a system for placing students into various tiers of support depending upon the severity of their needs. Often the framework includes Tier 1, which encompasses all students, and then two or more tiers of support that are provided only to below-benchmark students at different levels of intensity, depending upon need. A key piece of an effective MTSS framework is the assessment of below-benchmark students to pinpoint the deficits that are causing the difficulties. The resulting data provide a much-needed diagnosis before any decision on the types of targeted interventions to use. Students are assessed again to determine if the intervention is working and to decide on how to adjust the intervention to make it more effective; this process is referred to as "progress monitoring."

Another principle of MTSS is that *all* students receive what they need. Not only do the students who are furthest behind get additional minutes of intervention, but students who are at and above benchmark receive instruction that is differentiated for them as well.

Here is a definition of MTSS from the California Department of Education website (http://www.cde.ca.gov/ci/cr/ri/mtsscomprti2.asp) as of July 2017:

> In California, MTSS is an integrated, comprehensive framework that focuses on CCSS, core instruction, differentiated learning, student-centered learning, individualized student needs, and the alignment of systems necessary for all students' academic, behavioral, and social success. California has a long history of providing numerous systems of support. These include the interventions within the RtI[2] processes, supports for Special Education, Title I, Title III, support services for English Learners, American-Indian students, and those in gifted and talented programs. MTSS offers the potential to create needed systematic change through intentional design and redesign of services and supports that quickly identify and match the needs of all students.

Similarities and Differences Between MTSS and RTI

Generally, MTSS is considered to be a more comprehensive framework than RTI. Below is a list from the California Department of Education's website that explains the differences between MTSS and RtI^2 (California's name for RTI):

MTSS Differences with RtI^2

MTSS has a broader scope than does RtI^2. MTSS also includes:

- Focusing on aligning the entire system of initiatives, supports, and resources.
- Promoting district participation in identifying and supporting systems for alignment of resources, as well as site and grade level.
- Systematically addressing support for all students, including gifted and high achievers.
- Enabling a paradigm shift for providing support and setting higher expectations for all students through intentional design and redesign of integrated services and supports, rather than selection of a few components of RtI and intensive interventions.
- Endorsing Universal Design for Learning instructional strategies so all students have opportunities for learning through differentiated content, processes, and product.
- Integrating instructional and intervention support so that systemic changes are sustainable and based on CCSS-aligned classroom instruction.
- Challenging all school staff to change the way in which they have traditionally worked across all school settings.

MTSS is not designed for consideration in special education placement decisions, such as specific learning disabilities. MTSS focuses on all students in education contexts.

MTSS Similarities to RtI^2

MTSS incorporates many of the same components of RtI^2, such as

- Supporting high-quality standards and research-based, culturally and linguistically relevant instruction with the belief that every student can learn including students of poverty, students with disabilities, English learners, and students from all ethnicities evident in the school and district cultures.
- Integrating a data collection and assessment system, including universal screening, diagnostics and progress monitoring, to inform decisions appropriate for each tier of service delivery.

- Relying on a problem-solving systems process and method to identify problems, develop interventions, and evaluate the effectiveness of the intervention in a multitiered system of service delivery.
- Seeking and implementing appropriate research-based interventions for improving student learning.
- Using schoolwide and classroom research-based positive behavioral supports for achieving important social and learning outcomes.
- Implementing a collaborative approach to analyze student data and working together in the intervention process.

The Scope and Goal of This Book

The discussion of MTSS in this book is only about literacy. It doesn't include anything about MTSS in math or other academic areas, or as applied to behavior. In addition, this book focuses on literacy MTSS in elementary schools. Implementing MTSS in middle and high schools is different because student schedules are different, faculty are content specialists instead of generalists, and the structures are not the same as in elementary schools.

The goal of this book is to have educators evaluate their school's implementation of MTSS to see how it can be improved. MTSS is not new. Most elementary schools believe that they are already implementing MTSS in literacy. Yet results haven't been consistently strong. Many schools have had successes, although these spotlight examples are few and far between.

Be reflective and honest about whether your school's results are impressive. If they are not strong, determine the differences between your school's way of implementing MTSS and the approaches described in this book. Be willing to do things differently. MTSS implementation involves constantly evaluating, tweaking, and making changes. The work is never done. It's constantly evolving.

Overview of the Contents

Each of the book's 10 chapters relates to one of 10 success factors, expressed as recommendations for things to do:

1. Group by Skill Deficit
2. Use Diagnostic Assessments
3. Implement a Walk-to-Intervention Delivery Model
4. Monitor Progress with an Appropriate Assessment
5. Flood the Intervention Block with Extra Instructors

6. Use Intervention Time Wisely
7. Be Aware of What Makes Intervention Effective
8. Provide Teachers with Intervention Lesson Materials
9. Invest in Professional Development
10. Inspect What You Expect

An overarching element in this book is the understanding that teaching a child to read is both a science and an art. Let's look at the science part first.

An amazing thing about reading is that it's possible to pinpoint what a student can and can't do and figure out exactly what that student needs. An absolutely stunning amount of science addresses what skills students need to have by a certain point in time in order to learn to read. Scientific research shows the progression of stepping stones to learning to read, and which instructional practices work best for the students who struggle. Teachers don't have to guess about this. Best practice is to diagnose what skills a student hasn't yet mastered and then figure out a treatment plan. Treatment follows a good diagnosis.

Teaching reading is also an art—in various ways. I have deep respect for teachers who exhibit the art of teaching by motivating and connecting with students. Giving students feedback and observing what they just did wrong is also an art. There is no way to prescribe exactly what explanation will lead to a child "getting it"; teachers develop an instinct for what to try when a student isn't learning. There is also an art in matching text to student interests so children *want* to read.

The chapters that follow provide specific information and guidance to help educators understand the science and develop the art of teaching students to read.

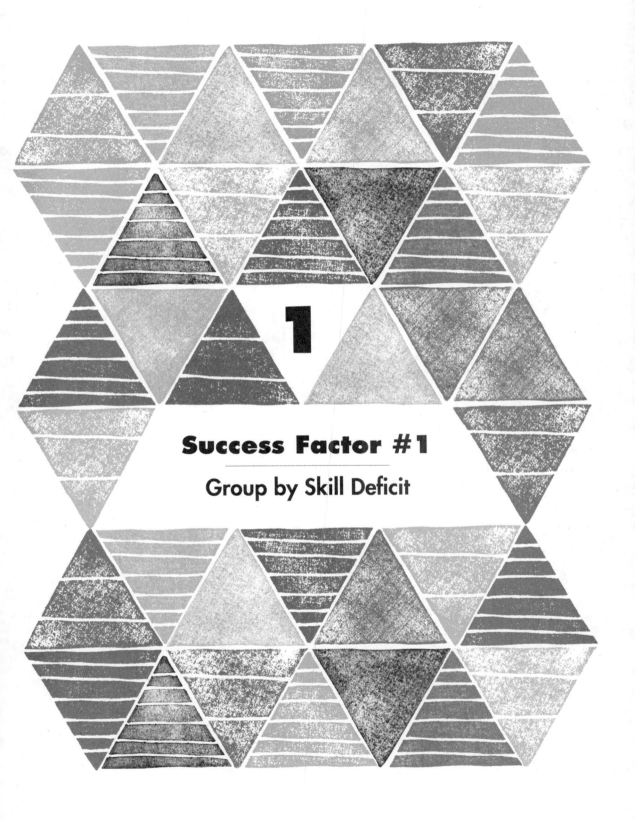

1

Success Factor #1

Group by Skill Deficit

One of the most important processes in MTSS is that of placing students in groups. Too often schools are using grouping processes that, from the outset, will limit potential student gains. The method of assigning students to groups makes *all* the difference in the results. A few key decisions drive results, and grouping is among the most important, which is why it is the first of the 10 factors for success.

An Early Experience in Forming Student Groups

In the early 2000s, eight schools in northwest Indiana participated in an early-reading initiative to provide professional development and materials to kindergarten and 1st grade teachers. Approximately 60 teachers gathered once a month for full-day workshops as participants in this effort, which was funded by a private foundation. The initiative's goal was to promote early identification and intervention for students who entered kindergarten unprepared to learn to read or who throughout kindergarten and 1st grade weren't making progress in acquiring the precursor and early skills needed to learn to read. Teachers received training on how to administer and score the Dynamic Indicators of Basic Early Literacy Skills (DIBELS) universal screening assessment, how to interpret the data and place students in groups, and how to teach strategies in small groups. This initiative took place just after the National Reading Panel's report, *Teaching Children to Read*, was released in 2000, before the federal Reading First program had reached full swing.

Funding of this Indiana initiative enabled the hiring of two people part-time. As one of those hired, my role was to design the program and teach the monthly workshops; the second person was an experienced reading coach named Iris who visited each school between the workshops and modeled instruction for the teachers. Iris was amazingly talented. She had worked with

Title I students in Atlanta, Georgia, before moving to Indiana. Watching Iris work with small groups of students not only taught the teachers a lot but also allowed me to see many things that were working and not working. She was a major reason the program was so successful and helped influence the direction of my future work.

One of the most important lessons I learned was about forming intervention groups. At the start of the school year, students were grouped based on whether their scores resulted in a DIBELS categorization designated by the colors yellow or red, indicating the level of intervention needed. Teachers were instructed to look at all the kids in the yellow category and form groups of three to four students based on which students worked best together. This was common practice at that time.

One day while watching Iris work with a group of four kindergartners, my gut was telling me that something was wrong. Iris was laying out pictures of a man, a mouse, and a ball. After saying the name of each picture, she'd ask the students to tell her which picture didn't fit in the /m/ category. (A letter appearing between slash marks indicates the sound pronounced instead of the letter name.) One girl we'll call Amy was nailing every question Iris asked. She already knew it. Why was Amy in this group? A review of Amy's DIBELS scoring booklet led to one of those "aha" moments early in my work. Amy's score was above benchmark on Initial Sound Fluency, so why was she in the yellow benchmark level? She was above benchmark for that skill, but she didn't know her letter names. Amy's very low score on letter naming overshadowed her strong skills in hearing initial sounds in words. Because the benchmark level is determined by a weighted average that includes both of these skills, the method of grouping was placing students in groups to get instruction they didn't need.

Watching misplaced students like Amy showed that our grouping practices weren't good enough. A quest to do better led to a new process. The next month we showed up at the workshop with two grouping mats formatted as 2 × 2 grids. One mat was for the middle of the year (MOY) of kindergarten, and the other mat was for 1st grade MOY. Each mat had one indicator on the horizontal axis and another one on the vertical axis. Because there was a benchmark and below-benchmark level for each indicator, the mats were divided into four boxes. Teachers reviewed their students' DIBELS scoring booklets and placed names in the four boxes based on high or low scores in each measure. The benchmark status levels of yellow and red identified the students whose booklets would be examined to place them in one of the four boxes, but those categories were no longer used for group placement. Sometimes a student whose level was red and another whose level was yellow would be in the same group.

The teachers returned to their schools and started meeting with their new groups. During the next couple of months, Iris and I observed the groups formed with this new approach. Not only did the teachers report that the students seemed to fit together better, but the progress-monitoring data showed larger gains than had been achieved with our previous grouping approach.

What about students scoring at benchmark levels? A common belief was that these students, who were in the green group, didn't need small-group intervention. This conclusion simply wasn't always accurate. For a handful of students whose weighted average composite score placed them at the benchmark level, the details in the scoring probes showed major deficits that could cause them to be below benchmark in the future if the deficits were not addressed. As they say, the devil is in the details. Therefore, back in the early 2000s our advice for teachers was to review students with benchmark composite scores to make sure that they were on track in all skills that would be important later. We paid especially close attention to students whose scores were barely in the benchmark range; we called these students "fence sitters."

This experience led to one major insight: the weighted average composite score that determines benchmark status levels can mask important details about an underlying deficit. Therefore, grouping based on the green, yellow, and red benchmark score categories is not as effective as grouping based on skill deficits. When students are placed in groups simply because they have been assigned the same benchmark score level (intensive/red or strategic/yellow), the approach doesn't go deep enough to help us understand *why* a student isn't at benchmark.

> When students are placed in groups because they have the same benchmark score level, the approach doesn't go deep enough to help us understand *why* a student isn't at benchmark.

Changes in Terminology in Universal Screeners

In the early 2000s, color categories represented status levels that were often called Benchmark (green), Strategic (yellow), and Intensive (red). The labels *Strategic* and *Intensive* were intended to describe how serious the intervention would need to be for the student to improve enough to reach the benchmark level. Many things have changed since then. There is a different version of DIBELS called DIBELS Next. And those category names have changed over time to labels such as "Below Benchmark" and "Well Below Benchmark." Figure 1.1 shows previous and current terminology.

FIGURE 1.1
Previous and Current Terms Used in DIBELS Universal Screeners

Color Coding	Previous Term	Current Term
Blue		Well Above Benchmark
Green	Benchmark	At or Above Benchmark
Yellow	Strategic	Below Benchmark
Red	Intensive	Well Below Benchmark

Common Grouping Practices and Why They Aren't Effective

The goal of grouping for intervention is to create groups that are tightly formed based on students' common skill deficit. Without good practices for group placement, it's impossible for the instructor to address a student's needs, especially because group time for intervention is typically only 30 minutes daily. Let's look at some common practices and why they are not producing robust results.

Grouping by Benchmark Score Level (Green, Yellow, Red)

Using an example of a classroom report from a universal screener for the middle of the year in kindergarten, let's see what happens if students are placed in the same group based on their benchmark score level on the composite score. First, let's review the names of the skills assessed in kindergarten. There are four indicators measured at this time of year for this grade level, and one indicator has two separate scores:

- **FSF—First Sound Fluency** (sometimes called Initial Sound Fluency): Assesses a student's ability to say the first sound in a word the assessor pronounces orally (without seeing print).
- **LNF—Letter Naming Fluency:** Assesses a student's ability to name letters while looking at them printed on a sheet (letters on page).
- **PSF—Phoneme Segmentation Fluency:** Assesses a student's ability to separately say each sound in a spoken word (no print).
- **NWF—Nonsense Word Fluency:** Assesses a student's ability to look at nonsense words and read them as if they are real words (nonsense words on page). There are two scores for this indicator:
  - **CLS—Correct Letter Sounds:** The ability to pronounce the correct sound for each letter in the nonsense word.
  - **WWR—Whole Words Read:** The ability to read the nonsense word as a whole word with all the sounds blended together.

Notice in Figure 1.2 that all five students are Below Benchmark (indicated with the yellow color coding) because their composite scores range from 85 to 116 points, and the minimum benchmark score is 122. Although these five students are all in the Below Benchmark category, they achieved this level in very different ways. Ashley scored below benchmark (yellow) on both phonemic awareness measures, FSF and PSF. In NWF, she scored at benchmark in reading letter sounds (CLS); however, she didn't read any whole words correctly (NWF WWR). Maria scored nearly the same as Ashley on the NWF CLS and was 10 points above benchmark on FSF and 1 point above on PSF.

Ashley needs more instruction on phonemic awareness, and given her low score on FSF, she probably should start with an early skill and work up. Maria is ready to focus on how to read blended words. With the proper focused instruction, Maria will most likely progress rapidly and be blending words quickly. Yet if the instruction starts at the phonemic awareness level that Ashley needs, Maria will be held back compared to the progress she could make if she skipped what she already knows and focused on what she needs now.

A concern about placing these five students together is how to determine an instructional focus that meets the needs of all of them. Most of the students need work on phoneme segmentation fluency (PSF)—especially Jose, who

FIGURE 1.2
Sample Classroom Report for Kindergarten, Middle of Year

Student Name	Benchmark					
	30–42	n/a	20–43	17–27	n/a	122–155
	FSF	LNF	PSF	NWF CLS	NWF WWR	Composite
Ashley	27 (yellow)	26	12 (yellow)	20 (green)	0	85 (yellow)
Jose	40 (green)	19	8 (red)	28 (green)	0	95 (yellow)
Kate	35 (green)	36	11 (yellow)	22 (green)	0	104 (yellow)
Maria	40 (green)	32	20 (green)	18 (green)	0	110 (yellow)
Sam	44 (green)	41	11 (yellow)	20 (green)	3	116 (yellow)

scored only 8 on that indicator. However, that approach would not be a good use of time for Maria, who is clearly at benchmark in both measures of phonemic awareness (FSF and PSF). Maria's focus should be on learning to read words. This example demonstrates why grouping by benchmark score level just doesn't work well.

One thing that bothers me is to hear students referred to as "red kids" or "yellow kids." A more sensitive phrase would be "kids in the red group." This advice is aligned with the sensitivity of person-first references for students who are receiving special education services. Rather than referring to "a dyslexic student," for example, we refer to "a student with dyslexia." The learning disability doesn't define the student's life but, rather, is just one aspect of it.

Grouping by Quadrants

I previously mentioned the idea of grouping by quadrants, an approach that is not based on composite scores. Students are placed in groups based on whether they score high or low on two specific indicators. During the Indiana literacy initiative, teachers studied their DIBELS student scoring booklets to place students in one of four quadrants based on their scores on two individual measures. Students who were at benchmark on the vertical and horizontal axis were placed in the upper-right quadrant. Students who scored low on both skills were placed in the lower-left quadrant. The other two quadrants were for students who were low on one and high on the other.

Fast-forwarding to today, this quadrant-grouping method is available in some of the data management systems that are used for collection and reporting of assessment data. Three popular systems are available for DIBELS reporting:

- DIBELSnet, from Dynamic Measurement Group (DMG), the authors of DIBELS
- UO DIBELS Data System, from the University of Oregon Center on Teaching and Learning
- mCLASS:DIBELS Next, from Amplify

The table in Figure 1.3 shows the two key indicators included in the grouping worksheets in DMG's DIBELSnet system. If the quadrant approach to grouping was used with the five kindergarten students in our example, they would be grouped as shown in Figure 1.4.

FIGURE 1.3
Two Key Indicators for Initial Grouping Worksheets in DIBELSnet

Grade Level	BOY (Beginning of Year)	MOY (Middle of Year)	EOY (End of Year)
Kindergarten	1. FSF 2. Composite Score	1. PSF 2. NWF CLS	1. PSF 2. NWF CLS
1st Grade	1. PSF 2. NWF CLS	1. NWF WWR 2. DORF Words Correct	1. NWF WWR 2. DORF Words Correct
2nd Grade	1. NWF WWR 2. DORF Words Correct	1. DORF Accuracy % 2. DORF Words Correct	1. DORF Accuracy % 2. DORF Words Correct
3rd Grade	1. DORF Accuracy % 2. DORF Words Correct	1. DORF Accuracy % 2. DORF Words Correct	1. DORF Accuracy % 2. DORF Words Correct
4th–6th Grade	1. DORF Accuracy % 2. DORF Words Correct	1. DORF Accuracy % 2. DORF Words Correct	1. DORF Accuracy % 2. DORF Words Correct

Source: Dynamic Measurement Group. Used with permission.

FIGURE 1.4

Quadrant Approach to Grouping Five Kindergarten Students

Indicator	Low PSF	High PSF
High NWF CLS	**Group 1**–Phonemic Awareness Intervention Ashley Jose Kate	**Group 2**–Benchmark
Low NWF CLS	**Group 3**–Intervention in Both Phoneme Segmentation and Letter-Sound Knowledge (PSF & NWF CLS)	**Group 4**–Intervention in Letter-Sound Knowledge (NWF CLS) Maria Sam

Quadrant grouping provides better results than grouping by merely using the benchmark level. Preparing quadrants is fast and easy and certainly a good start. Dynamic Measurement Group even refers to it as "Initial Grouping" to indicate that the teacher must further revise these groupings based on other information about students' skill levels, available resources, and magnitude of student need. I recommended the quadrant-grouping approach in the first edition of *I've DIBEL'd, Now What?* (Hall, 2006). Yet there's an even better way to group, which will be explored in Chapter 2. It requires using a diagnostic assessment instrument.

Outcomes of an Ineffective Grouping Process

Ineffective grouping processes lead to the following outcomes:

- Mixture of needs in the same group
- Lack of clarity about exactly which skills have been mastered and which are deficient
- Difficulty selecting appropriate instructional materials
- Unclear goals for the group
- Challenge in determining the best instrument to measure progress

These outcomes make clear why ineffective grouping processes can have such a negative effect on the chances of success in implementing MTSS.

Why DIBELS Is Prevalent in This Book

This book includes many references to DIBELS because DIBELS represents the category of universal screeners known as Curriculum-Based Measures (CBMs). DIBELS has been a popular assessment used by many schools throughout the United States, especially during the days of Reading First. Although educators today use many assessments and I don't advocate any one in particular, a discussion of assessments requires specifics. Therefore, I use DIBELS as an example of a universal screening assessment.

Many other assessments use indicators to predict overall reading achievement by assessing a limited number of skills as proxies for an entire area of skills. In addition, many assessments use levels with names similar to Benchmark, Below Benchmark, and Well Below Benchmark. Many assessments also use the green, yellow, and red color-coding to represent where students fall.

Why Universal Screeners Don't Provide Enough Data to Group by Skill Deficits

A key to successful MTSS results is tight grouping. When the word *tight* precedes the phrase *skill groups*, it means that all students in the group need to work on the same specific skill, so instructional time will be equally effective for each of them. The skill is not a broad area, such as "phonological awareness" or "phonics." For example, a kindergarten group is not composed to work on phonological awareness or even phonemic awareness but, rather, the specific skill within phonemic awareness—such as *phoneme segmentation*. Every minute of instruction is important, and because it's delivered in a small-group format, it's expensive. Instructional time has the potential to enable struggling readers to learn something they're missing. To be effective, student grouping has to be carefully designed.

Tier 2 and Tier 3 groups in an MTSS framework provide valuable time for struggling readers. Because whole-class instruction typically encompasses more than 20 students, it's impossible for the teacher to provide each student with specific feedback during this time. Therefore, what happens during the Tier 2 and Tier 3 small-group time really matters in terms of the results achieved in MTSS.

Universal screeners have a distinct purpose, and they do a great job in achieving that purpose. They are designed to assess all students multiple times a year to see if they are on track, or at benchmark, at a specific time of the year—for example, BOY (beginning of the year), MOY (middle of the year), or EOY (end of the year)—in a designated grade level. Because these assessments are given to all students multiple times a year and most are administered one-on-one, they have to be completed in a limited number of minutes. They are designed with a few key indicators to predict overall reading achievement, which means that only a few skills—typically anywhere from two to five—are measured each time.

The authors who design universal screeners select which skills to measure based not on the most important skills for reading development but on the skills that best predict later reading achievement. For example, as noted earlier in this chapter, one of the skills measured in kindergarten is Letter Naming Fluency. It's not necessary for students to say the letter names to be able to read. What they do have to do is to look at a letter and say the sound while blending words. If letter-sound knowledge is more important than letter naming for reading, then why do nearly all the universal screeners measure letter naming? They do so because letter naming in kindergarten is predictive of who will read later. Letter naming seems to be a great proxy of kindergarten readiness. Children who come to kindergarten knowing letter names are often those who participated in high-quality preschool programs or were raised in households where parents or caregivers took the time to teach the child letter names.

Because the purpose of a universal screener is to quickly figure out which students are on track through measurement three times a year, the screener must be quick to administer. Therefore, typically there's only one indicator measured for each literacy area. Even if two skills are measured, they still may not provide enough information to show teachers where to start intervention.

Let's look at phonological awareness (PA), where often two areas are measured in kindergarten and 1st grade: First Sound Fluency (also called Initial Sound Fluency) and Phoneme Segmentation Fluency. Both measure phoneme-level skills, which is one of three levels of PA. When a student is low on one or both phonemic awareness measures, a teacher still doesn't know whether to go back to the syllable or the rime level as a starting point for instruction. Although assessing syllable awareness helps determine a starting point for students who are below benchmark, the extra time can't be justified for benchmark students.

As noted in the Introduction, teaching reading is an art and a science. One of the scientific aspects is the fact that research has clarified the order of skill development. Experts talk about the development of skills from phonological awareness to phonics to reading connected text fluently. There are well-researched sequences within several of these essential components of reading instruction. For example, according to research, phonological awareness develops from the syllable level to the onset-rime level to the phoneme level. The order of phonics instruction is also placed in a sequence from the easier to the more complex skills. Children are typically taught short- and long-vowel patterns before vowel teams or *r*-controlled vowels.

To group by skill deficits, it's essential to think in terms of a sequence of skills and to pinpoint where a student is in his development. If he can't get a benchmark score on Phoneme Segmentation Fluency, how is he on syllables and rhyming words? Think in terms of where he has mastery and where he is failing. Universal screeners do a great job at what they are designed to do. But if a student isn't at benchmark on the universal screener, the work is not done. It's critical to pick apart the skills one at a time, and that can't be done with a universal screener. That's why diagnostic assessments—the topic of Chapter 2—are necessary.

> The most effective approach is to place students in groups by specific skill deficits, which means the teacher can clearly see what to teach.

Summing Up

Placement of students into small groups is a critical success factor in MTSS. Schools experiencing success are ensuring that the groups are skill based. A less effective grouping method is based on whether the student's universal screener composite score places him in the Below Benchmark or Well Below Benchmark status. Another common approach is to group from the universal screener indicators through a quadrant approach. This approach is better than the benchmark-level approach, but still not the optimum. The most effective approach is to place students in groups by specific skill deficits, which means all the students in a group need pretty much the same thing, and the teacher can clearly see what to teach.

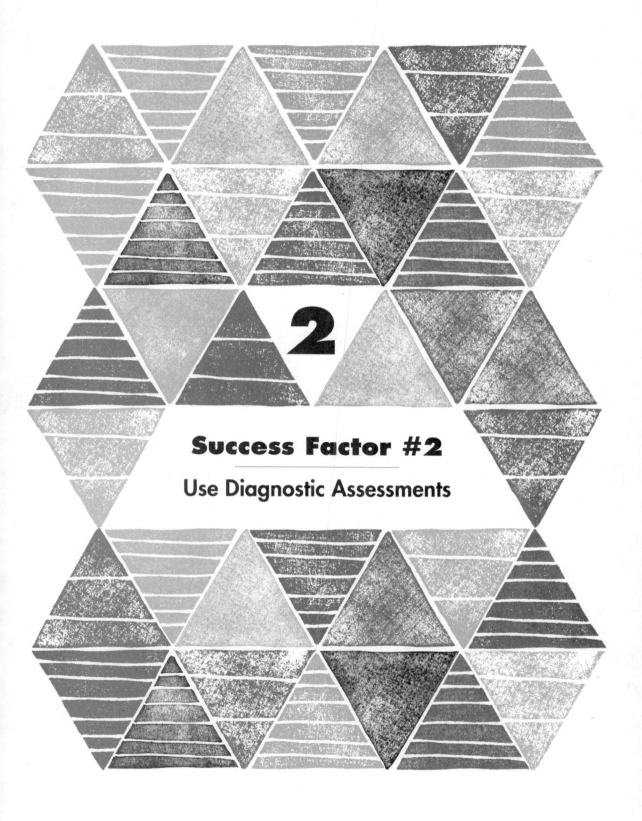

2

Success Factor #2

Use Diagnostic Assessments

Chapter 1 focused on why grouping students by skill deficit is a key to achieving the best results with MTSS. The issue is that many schools are using the wrong assessment data to look at skill deficits. Universal screener data do not provide an adequate drill-down to the skill-level information needed to place students in appropriate skill groups. Chapter 1 described two possible approaches to grouping with universal screener data—quadrant grouping and grouping based on benchmark status level—neither of which leads to tight enough skill groups. Both approaches have drawbacks. The quadrant grouping approach is preferable to grouping based on benchmark status level (which uses composite scores that are weighted averages of indicators) because a student's strengths and weaknesses are captured—at least for the subskills measured and included on the quadrant. Although the quadrant approach is preferable, it still isn't good enough because not enough skills are measured.

For optimum grouping, schools need diagnostic assessment data. The purpose of Chapter 2 is to explain how a diagnostic assessment is different from three other types of assessments—universal screeners, progress-monitoring assessments, and outcome assessments—and to describe the characteristics of a good diagnostic assessment. Not only do diagnostic assessments provide the necessary data, but using them helps teachers develop a diagnostic mindset for pinpointing *how* to help struggling readers.

Diagnostic assessment is the gateway to being able to group by skill deficit, which is probably the most essential requirement for robust results. I am reminded of an incident at the conclusion of a conference where I was presenting at a breakout session. A participant approached me and said that her school was one of the first pilot RTI schools in Washington State. She said, "We aren't getting the results you describe. We have so many pieces, but our teachers aren't doing skill groups. We don't have diagnostic assessments. This was the reason that I came to this conference. Now I know what we're missing."

Confusion about the types and purposes of different assessments is prevalent. When presenting at conference sessions, my 95 Percent Group colleagues and I frequently ask for a show of hands as to whether the participants have access to diagnostic assessments in their schools. In response, somewhere between 10 and 50 percent of the participants raise their hands, depending upon the location of the conference. This absence of diagnostic assessments is a key reason for the lackluster results from MTSS.

> Diagnostic assessment is the gateway to being able to group by skill deficit, which is probably the most essential requirement for robust results.

In describing different assessments, I like to compare them to different types of bicycles. My family loves to ride mountain bikes in Arizona. Our adult son is a serious cyclist. He doesn't have a lot of furniture or clothes, but he owns five bikes. He explains that he needs a different bike for each type of cycling he enjoys. Although it's hard to fully understand how each bike is unique, let's look at two contrasting types of bikes he rides, as illustrated in Figure 2.1.

The bike on the left is called a mountain bike. The one on the right is a road bike. There are some very important differences between these bicycles. Consider these questions:

- Which one has fatter tires?
- Which one has a lighter frame?
- Which bike has a suspension system?
- On which bike is the rider sitting straight up?

The road bike has a lighter frame and thinner tires with less tread. The mountain bike has fatter tires with more treads, as well as a suspension system to enable the rider to be more comfortable when riding over rough terrain. Most mountain bikes have a heavier frame than a road bike.

How do the differences relate to their purposes? Road bikes are designed to be ridden on smooth pavement at fast speeds. The design of the bike, with its

FIGURE 2.1
Comparing a Mountain Bike and a Road Bike

Source: Bike photos courtesy of Trek Bikes. Reprinted with permission.

sleek look and feel, supports that type of riding. Riders sit in an aerodynamic position, leaning over and grasping the curved handlebars. Mountain bikes, which are built to ride off-road on trails with rough terrain, have heavier, softer tires with more-visible treads that grip the rough surface. The trails are rocky and winding, and there are often ruts caused when rainwater cuts grooves in the dirt. Many trails are a single track close to rocks, trees, bushes, cacti, and other plants. On Arizona trails, a fall can mean landing on a prickly cactus. (Did you know that most Arizona mountain bikers carry tweezers in their pack along with a spare tire?) Riding a road bike with those skinny tires on the trails in Arizona wouldn't be fun. The rider would risk falling because the thinner tires can more easily get caught in ruts and tip the bike over. The thin tires on road bikes would also puncture more easily, which would mean stopping more often to change a tire. Thank goodness for a slimy green compound that we've applied to our mountain bike tires that keeps them inflated when the cactus needles poke small holes in them!

Four Types of Assessments

Like bikes, assessments come in various types, and the design follows the purpose. Just as a mountain bike is designed for a different kind of riding than a road bike, universal screeners are designed differently than diagnostic assessments because their purpose is different. The success of a school's MTSS is dependent upon effective use of appropriate data. One contribution of the professional development for Reading First was the foundational knowledge that educators gained about the four different types of reading assessments (universal screeners, diagnostic assessments, progress-monitoring assessments, and outcome assessments). Regardless of whether any other aspect of Reading First was viewed as successful, there is general agreement that the professional development was outstanding. Unfortunately, only a limited number of schools in the United States got to participate. As a result, most U.S. teachers and administrators know very little about these assessment types.

As discussed in Chapter 1, attempting to use universal screener data to group students is like trying to fit a square peg into a round hole. Nevertheless, many schools do exactly this because they lack the foundational knowledge about assessment types. Teachers don't know much about how to evaluate assessments and identify which ones provide the kind of data that is optimal for forming groups. Unfortunately, the proliferation of assessments over the last 10 to 15 years has not been accompanied by a parallel amount of training for administrators and teachers on understanding the different types and purposes of assessments.

Many schools have multiple assessments in one category and no assessments in another category. The key questions to ask about assessments are these:

- What do they tell me?
- Why and when do I use each one?
- What are the four types of assessment?
- How do I use the data from each assessment type to inform instructional decisions?

The next sections present an overview of the four types of assessments. We then explore diagnostic assessments in depth, because this type is essential for an effective school implementation of MTSS.

Assessment Type #1: Universal Screeners

The first type of assessment, the universal screener, is a brief assessment that identifies which students are at benchmark by measuring indicators that are predictive of later reading achievement. This assessment is administered to all, or nearly all, students (hence the name *universal*) several times a year, such as at the beginning, middle, and end of the year, to determine if they are progressing along the path of reading development to stay at or above benchmark level.

One of the most common types of universal screeners is called a Curriculum-Based Measure (CBM). These screeners are individually administered. An assessor listens to a student provide letter sounds, provide letter names, or read passages aloud, depending upon the grade level. The assessor records mistakes and stops the student when the allotted time is over. Standardized instructions are read precisely as written each time the screener is administered. All universal screeners score the number of correct answers within a time period—a minute, for example—so all the indicators include the word *fluency*.

A student's score on a universal screener is compared to a benchmark score. Benchmark levels are determined by collecting data for large groups of students that are reflective of the nation's demographics. Universal screeners use indicators at one point in time to predict later reading success. Based on how well a child does on selected indicators at this point, the screener predicts success on the next step up. The entire design is based on predicting an individual child's likelihood of later success in reading based on looking at what strong readers were able to do at this stage, on these measures. Children who make this benchmark have a high likelihood of reaching the next level up.

It's important to understand how the assessment authors select which indicators to include. The ones that make the cut are those that are most predictive from one period to the next. The selection criterion is based not on the most important things for reading development but, rather, on which indicators are most predictive from one point to the next. An indicator that is highly predictive at one point can lose its power of prediction as time goes on. For example, Phoneme Segmentation Fluency (PSF) is a strong predictor at the end of kindergarten but loses its potency once a child is reading words in 1st grade.

One assessment author explains in workshops that a universal screener is like poking a toothpick in a cake to determine if it is sufficiently baked. When the toothpick comes out clean, without any batter clinging to it, the cake is ready to remove from the oven to cool. Chefs typically poke the toothpick not only in the center—because it's the last part to finish baking—but also in a couple of other places to ensure that the cake's uniformly baked. Although poking in more places would give more perfect information, a cake with too many holes wouldn't be very appealing. Poking it in a couple of spots is an indicator of whether the rest of the cake is done. Similarly, the universal screener indicators estimate the overall level of reading achievement without measuring them all, which would take too much time.

A variety of reports show the data from different perspectives. One of the most popular reports lists all the students in a classroom and displays their score on each indicator, whether that score reaches benchmark for that time, and their composite score. (Figure 1.2 in Chapter 1 is an example of such a report.) Other reports display entire grade levels to review the percentage of students at each benchmark score level (At or Above Benchmark, Below Benchmark, or Well Below Benchmark). Then there are reports that roll data up for an entire district. Reports not only look at different groups, such as a classroom or an entire grade level, but also can be prepared to review a single point in time or growth across periods, like beginning of year (BOY) to middle of year (MOY).

Teaching to a universal screener is a mistake. Although the indicators in this test are important skills, they are not the only skills that matter. Because the assessment must be administered in a minimum amount of time, many important skills are not measured, giving teachers only limited visibility into the full complement of steps along the way to success as a reader. Although the selected indicators are statistically good predictors of overall later reading levels, they by no means signal that only these skills need to be taught for all to be well.

Let's consider an example that illustrates the difference between what's assessed and what's taught. In 1st grade, most CBMs measure Phoneme Segmentation Fluency (at the beginning of the year), Nonsense Word Fluency, Oral Reading Fluency, and Retell. Grade 1 NWF prompts include short-vowel words in the consonant-vowel-consonant (CVC) and vowel-consonant (VC) patterns. Nonsense words such as *sim, lut, vit,* and *op* are NWF examples. Here are additional skills beyond CVC and VC that 1st graders need to master, along with example words:

- Consonant blends with short vowels (*sand, stop*)
- Consonant digraphs with short vowels (*ship, this, chick*)
- Long vowel silent-*e* (*make, luge*)

Although words with these patterns are found in the passages that students read orally, the only word types measured separately in the NWF measure are VC and CVC words. Students would be far behind if they left 1st grade having mastered only VC and CVC words.

Assessment Type #2: Diagnostic Assessments

The second type of assessment, the diagnostic assessment, is designed to dive deeply into one area. Excellent diagnostic assessments are available to measure skill acquisition in two areas: phonological awareness and phonics. At this time, no diagnostic assessments provide the information needed in the areas of comprehension or vocabulary. Note that in this book this category is referred to as diagnostic *assessments* and not diagnostic *screeners* to further distinguish it from universal screeners.

A diagnostic assessment isn't designed to provide a comprehensive view of reading achievement; it's a snapshot of one area, but a more extensive one than is provided by a universal screener. If a universal screener skims across a lake, dipping down a bit into a few areas, a diagnostic assessment hovers over just one area and dives deeply to explore it to the bottom of the lake.

The universal screener tells you *who* is not at benchmark. The diagnostic tells you *why* a student isn't reading at benchmark and what to do about it. When looking at a classroom report from a universal screener, a teacher can readily see who is at benchmark and who is not. The students not at benchmark pop out because their composite scores are at or below the benchmark threshold level. Its purpose is to identify which students are at risk of not achieving expected levels of performance for the indicators to be measured at later times. Schools getting the best results realize that the job is not done once a universal screener is administered. Any student *not* at benchmark needs more assessment, but now with a diagnostic tool instead of the universal screener.

Diagnostic assessments need to be given to only some students. The students making adequate progress on achieving literacy milestones don't need to be assessed with diagnostic instruments. In spite of repeated assurances of this, it's amazing to return for coaching visits and hear teachers confessing that they gave the diagnostic assessment to *all* their students because the data were so insightful that they wanted the information for everyone in their class.

Typical practice is to administer a diagnostic assessment after universal screening only to students who score below benchmark and whose universal screening data point to a deficit in an area that can be measured with a diagnostic assessment. The purpose of the diagnostic analysis is to learn more about what a student can and can't do in a particular area to inform decisions about the best instructional approach. Once struggling students' individual deficits are pinpointed, the students can be placed in skill groups and instructional materials can be selected to address specific needs. If the school isn't going to differentiate intervention instruction, then diagnostic assessment is a waste of time. Failure to differentiate intervention instruction for each struggling reader reveals a fundamental misunderstanding of the principles of MTSS.

The medical model offers a great analogy to good MTSS assessment practices. When a patient enters the emergency room or an internist's office, the first thing a nurse does is capture a small set of indicators. The nurse, often called a triage nurse, takes the patient's blood pressure, temperature, and pulse. These three measures are used to determine the level of urgency and to essentially place patients in categories such as "strategic" and "intensive." The patients whose indicators show the highest risk are whisked into an examination room to be seen by a doctor ahead of those whose indicators show lower risk conditions. These indicators, along with the patient's reported level of pain, lead to more assessment. The next step is diagnostic assessment to figure out the specific cause of the medical issue. It would be considered malpractice if a medical professional gave a patient a prescription without a clear diagnosis. The treatment plan follows, pinpointing the cause via a thorough diagnosis.

The procedure is much the same with struggling readers. It's ineffective practice to go straight from a universal screener to determining intervention instruction without a good diagnostic evaluation in between. If teachers skip that middle step, it's not possible to know what group a student should be in and which lessons will address the issue. As noted earlier, the universal screener tells you *who* didn't reach benchmark, and the diagnostic assessment tells you *why* and *what* to do about it. Diagnostic assessments are a necessity for appropriately placing struggling readers in intervention groups, and they are not expensive.

During workshops, one of the consultants in our company explains that the universal screener alerts teachers when the house is on fire. It can even alert them to how urgent the fire is. It may indicate how quickly the house is burning so the fire department knows how many fire trucks to send and whether a ladder truck is needed. The diagnostic evaluation tells which room the fire started in and how to put it out. It's essential to figure out the source of the fire; simply pouring water on it may not extinguish it, depending upon the type of fire.

Administering a Diagnostic Assessment

A diagnostic assessment is administered one-on-one, with the assessor listening to the student's pronunciation of the sounds and words and recording responses on a student recording sheet. Assessment can take less than 10 minutes per student if it is designed with skills in order from simplest to most complex. The assessment is discontinued when the student fails to pass a skill (or fails two in a row). Because the purpose is to determine the starting skill for intervention instruction, continuing administration of higher skills once a student fails at a lower point is unnecessary. With intervention, the student moves up the skills continuum until reaching the appropriate skill for a grade level. For example, if a 2nd grade student is below benchmark on phonics skills, intervention would continue through short vowels, long vowels, vowel teams, and r-controlled vowels but stop before syllable types because the core program provides plenty of instruction on those skills.

Although some researchers advise that timing a diagnostic assessment provides important information, as of today most are not timed. Not timing enables assessors to better record careful notes on a student's response, including by slowing the student down when needed or asking for a rereading to hear the response clearly. A good compromise might be to not time the assessment for group placement and then time the progress monitoring to determine if a student is ready to be exited from the skill group.

The assessment provides subskill scores so the teacher can see mastery on each separate skill. Mastery is generally defined as 80 percent or 90 percent correct to "pass" that skill. On a phonics diagnostic instrument, if a 1st grader "passes" short vowels in consonant-vowel-consonant words, then the next level may be short vowels with consonant blends. With a passing score on that level, he then tries short vowels with digraphs. Assessment continues until he cannot pass a skill. That skill becomes the starting point for intervention instruction.

Why Universal Screeners and Diagnostic Assessments Are Mutually Exclusive

If an assessment is a really good universal screener, it cannot be a diagnostic assessment. Each type is designed to serve a different purpose. Just as road bikes and mountain bikes are built for two completely different uses, so too are these assessments.

Universal screeners are designed to find out who's at benchmark and who's not. They are administered individually, multiple times a year, to the entire class, so they must take less than 15 minutes. Although only a few indicators are assessed, because a universal screener is given to all students periodically, the amount of time it takes to administer is critically important. In contrast, a diagnostic assessment is given only to some students and deeply examines only one reading component (phonemic awareness or phonics). Whereas the universal screener may measure only two phonemic awareness skills, a diagnostic assessment might measure up to 25 different skills within the PA area. If a student isn't at benchmark on the universal screener's phonemic awareness indicators, administering a PA diagnostic instrument helps pinpoint what the student has mastered, which skills are missing, and where to start the intervention instruction.

Again, the same assessment cannot be both a universal screener and a diagnostic assessment. If it's good for one purpose, it will be deficient for the other. To do a good job at diagnosis, it's necessary to assess baby steps along a continuum to observe mastery until the student can't pass a skill. If a universal screener tried to assess every step, it would take forever to administer. Teachers would be up in arms because of the time wasted in measuring all those steps for benchmark students. Universal screeners provide a look at overall reading levels, including decoding, reading fluency, and comprehension (for grades 1 and above). Diagnostics look at just one area, but all steps are measured rather than just the predictive indicators.

Appropriately placing students in Tier 2 and Tier 3 groups is so important for getting strong results. Struggling readers don't get a lot of time in small groups. Time is precious, and teaching them what they already know is a waste of everybody's time—something that schools can't afford. It's imperative to do a really good job of diagnosing before figuring out what the treatment plan should be.

Assessment Type #3: Progress-Monitoring Assessments

The purpose of progress monitoring, the third type of assessment, is to determine if a student who's receiving instruction is making progress. In many respects, it's like the "recalculating" voice of a GPS. Once students are placed in an initial group, it's the progress-monitoring data that inform decisions about when to exit a skill and which skill to address next. The course corrections that are part of the intervention journey require a cycle of teaching, testing, regrouping, teaching some more, assessing again, and so on. Progress-monitoring assessments guide teachers in making decisions about what to do next. Did it work? Has the student mastered a specific skill? Can we exit him from this group? What's the next skill he needs? The cycle goes on and on. The progress-monitoring data answer all those questions. Thank goodness guesswork is no longer required!

Administering a Progress-Monitoring Assessment

During workshops we're often asked the following question: Who should administer the progress-monitoring assessment? Our recommendation is that whoever is providing the instruction should give the progress-monitoring assessment. That way the instructor working with the student can watch him answering the probes. If it's a CBM (curriculum-based measure), then the assessment is given one-on-one, with the teacher listening to the student respond while recording the errors. (The diagnostic assessments envisioned here require the teacher to listen to the student pronounce sounds and read words or passages. Computer-based assessments can't do this.)

Another common question is this: How often should we monitor progress? Most schools choose a cycle of every two to three weeks, with more frequent assessment for students who are not making consistent progress. Although assessment frequency is important, an even more essential question is *which* assessment instrument to use.

Selecting an Appropriate Assessment for Progress Monitoring

Our recommendation is to use the assessment that most closely measures what you're teaching. Occasionally the best choice is an alternate form of one of

> The course corrections that are part of the intervention journey require a cycle of teaching, testing, regrouping, teaching some more, assessing again, and so on.

the universal screener indicators. For example, a good way to measure fluency improvements in reading connected text is to use an alternate form, or progress-monitoring passage, of an Oral Reading Fluency indicator in a universal screener. There are also alternate forms of Phoneme Segmentation Fluency indicators in a universal screener to monitor the progress of groups working on PSF.

For other skills, the instrument that's more aligned to the skill taught is frequently an alternate form of a diagnostic assessment. In this book, I recommend grouping by specific skill groups, and most of the time it's not possible to measure a particular skill with a CBM.

A lot of schools believe that they should monitor progress with their universal screener. Assuming it's DIBELS, that's fine for the few skills where the DIBELS indicators measure what you're teaching. The skills that can be measured well with DIBELS include fluency with an ORF passage, reading of consonant-vowel-consonant words with the Nonsense Word Fluency probe, and two phonemic awareness skills (First Sound Fluency and Phoneme Segmentation Fluency).

The vast majority of skills are better measured with an alternate form of a diagnostic assessment. Every once in a while it's useful to still check students with the universal screener. One option is to assess all kids in intervention two additional times with the universal screener—once between the fall and winter benchmark, and a second time between the winter and spring benchmark. This approach provides a calibration between the diagnostic and universal screener data.

Let's look at an example. Imagine that a student named Estelle is below benchmark on Oral Reading Fluency. Because phonics decoding appears to be an issue, a phonics diagnostic assessment is administered, and the data reveal that she knows all her short-vowel word patterns but misses long-vowel silent-*e* words. Estelle is placed in a Tier 2 group with other students needing instruction in this word pattern. After several weeks of instruction, Estelle's intervention teacher monitors her progress with the phonics diagnostic Form B section for long-vowel silent-*e*. If the teacher had monitored Estelle's progress with an Oral Reading Fluency passage, it would have been nearly impossible to tell if she was ready to move to her next missing skill because an ORF passage wouldn't have included enough silent-*e* words. The point is clear: it's key to select the assessment instrument that most closely measures the skill that's been the focus of instruction.

Assessment Type #4: Outcome Measures

One of the most common outcome measures—the fourth type of assessment—is the state-mandated assessment. The data tell whether students are reaching sufficient levels of achievement in literacy and mathematics, and they enable comparisons of districts and schools across a state. These assessments are typically aligned with a state's standards or the Common Core. As of 2018, some states are still using Smarter Balance and PARCC. Outcome measures are administered in a whole-group setting and often on computer systems. States usually designate testing days, when all students in a particular grade level in all schools statewide are assessed within a specific window of time.

Although the primary purpose is to look at achievement across a state, these assessments do provide some data about strengths and weaknesses of individual students. Because of their design, they are not useful for making instructional adjustments. Outcome measures are summative rather than formative assessments; they measure whether or not students have learned content or skills at the end of a specific period.

Using a Universal Screener and a Diagnostic Assessment Together

Earlier in this chapter, I mentioned the benefit of using a universal screener and a diagnostic assessment together. Let's look at an example of this with sample data for two 2nd grade students in September:

- Student 1, Jose, scored 52 words correct per minute (wcpm) on the DORF measure (DIBELS Oral Reading Fluency), which is at the very bottom of the benchmark range of 52–67.
- Student 2, Mary, scored 52 wcpm on the ORF measure, which is exactly the same as Jose's score.

Teachers typically do not look at only one indicator score—they look at the composite as well as the individual indicator scores, and they also look at the other indicators measured at this time of year. For this illustration, we'll focus on only the Oral Reading Fluency measure. Although both students got 52 wcpm, they shouldn't necessarily be in the same group.

It's critical to know how each of them got the score of 52—to know not only how many words they got correct but also how many they missed. That factor is measured by the accuracy rate, which is the percentage of accurate words in the total number read. Jose's accuracy rate was 99 percent, which is actually well above the benchmark range of 90 to 95 percent. On the other hand, Mary's accuracy rate was 79 percent, which is well below benchmark (0 percent to 80 percent). Mary read a lot more words but got a lot more wrong. These two students are not reading the same way—in spite of their identical wcpm scores. In earlier versions of curriculum-based measures like DIBELS and AIMSweb, the accuracy score was not calculated or considered in the composite scores. This important measurement is now included in the current versions of most CBM assessments.

What's the next step with these two students? Jose is fine for now, assuming that his composite score is At or Above Benchmark. If it isn't, then further analysis is needed. However, the story is different for Mary. Regardless of what her composite score is, with a "fence-sitter" score on Oral Reading Fluency and an accuracy rate in the Well Below Benchmark range, it is essential to do further diagnostic analysis. With an accuracy rate that low, administering a phonics diagnostic assessment is clearly the next step. Mary's teacher needs to know how well she can read words containing each of the phonics concepts that students at her grade level are expected to know. The goal is to pinpoint what she knows and where she's still deficient.

By the end of 1st grade, students are expected to be able to proficiently read one-syllable words with short vowels including consonant blends and digraphs, and words with the long vowel silent-*e* pattern. This includes words like those in the following list:

- Short vowel with consonant-vowel-consonant pattern: *man*, *pin*, *sun*
- Short vowel with consonant blend pattern: *hand*, *stop*
- Short vowel with consonant digraph pattern: *ship*, *chick*
- Long vowel with silent-*e* pattern: *lake*, *ride*, *mule*

If Mary is missing so many words when reading passages written specifically for beginning-of-the-year 2nd graders, it's possible she's still not fluently reading 1st grade words like those listed above. If her teacher tries to place her in an intervention group based on her universal screener data, she'd be just guessing as to what Mary needs. The best way to know what Mary has mastered and what she is proficient in is to observe how well she reads words with each of these patterns while giving her a phonics diagnostic assessment.

Because students can memorize simple words they have seen repeatedly, asking them to read lists of real words doesn't provide the diagnostic information teachers need. For this reason, diagnostic phonics assessments use nonsense words. Instead of asking a student to read the words *lake*, *ride*, or *rule*, asking her to read the nonsense words *sone*, *mive*, and *splate* will give the teacher a great deal more information about the student's ability to apply the concept to unfamiliar words. It's impossible to memorize every English word, and the ability to figure out how to read an unfamiliar word by applying the concept of the word pattern is crucial for fluent reading, especially when text complexity increases beyond the 1st grade level.

A school achieving mediocre MTSS gains may be placing students in a phonics group based on incomplete data. In addition, if the school's practice is to start each group on the same lesson and complete all lessons in a program, it is unlikely to be experiencing robust gains. Starting everyone on Lesson 1 and teaching through Lesson 99 is just inefficient. It's wasting the children's time. Diagnostic data are needed to differentiate the exact phonics patterns that the group needs.

Think about the MTSS assessment process as a kind of funnel. All students are screened with the school's universal screener—the wide end of the funnel. The purpose of that assessment is to determine who is not at benchmark and to get some insights on what area to probe next (phonological awareness, phonics, fluency, vocabulary, or comprehension). For the students who are not at benchmark—who do not pass through the funnel—the next step is to diagnose what the treatment plan should be. To do that, teachers will need good diagnostic data that enable pinpointing the lowest deficient skill. Where did the student start to have trouble? Which skill is the lowest in a progression from simple to complex?

In the next sections, we'll look at two diagnostic assessments, both of which are published by my company, 95 Percent Group. They are the *Phonics Screener for Intervention*™ (*PSI*™) and the *Phonological Awareness Screener for Intervention*™ (*PASI*™).

Phonics Diagnostic Assessments

Phonics diagnostic data provide the assessor with information about a student's ability to read words with phonics patterns, such as short vowels, long vowels, *r*-controlled vowels, and multisyllable words. Phonics diagnostics are generally quite brief. As informal evaluation instruments, phonics diagnostics are typically not norm-referenced or standardized. They are criterion-referenced with a minimum acceptable score necessary to consider a student at mastery level for each skill. The 95 Percent Group's *PSI* may be administered by any school staff member who has knowledge of phonics rules. While testing a student, the assessor not only marks student responses as correct or incorrect, but also carefully records student miscues or incorrect responses.

The assessment is administered one-on-one by a teacher sitting with a student. The student is looking at a sheet of paper with the prompts while the teacher listens and records information on a student scoring sheet. After going over the instructions, the student reads each prompt on the page. If the student seems not to understand what to do, the teacher can stop and explain the instructions in her own words. The assessment is not timed, so the teacher can stop the student and say, for example, "I need you to slow down so I can write down exactly what you say." Some students need to be asked to speak louder to be heard. These practices are not allowed while administering a universal screener, which is a standardized assessment and therefore requires reading the instructions exactly as written and not slowing down a student, because the number of answers given in one minute is part of the scoring.

Use of Nonsense Words in Phonics Diagnostic Assessments

Phonics diagnostic assessments typically include some of the following three things:

- Lists of nonsense words
- Lists of real words
- Real words in sentences

Two of the three are included in 95 Percent Group's *PSI*. Although it's possible to include all three, it's not necessary. To save time, isolated real words are excluded in the 95 Percent version. What we want to know is how the student does when presented with a word that hasn't been previously learned, which is best assessed with nonsense words. The most essential piece is to observe how the student reads a nonsense word when it's a word he can't recognize by sight. The 95 Percent *PSI* does include reading real words in sentences.

During the day, when teachers watch kids read passages, they are seeing how students read real words in the context of sentences. Assessing real words in sentences and nonsense words enables the teacher to see the contrast in scores between the two tasks. Sometimes teachers react with dismay at a low score on the nonsense word portion and exclaim, "But he's reading!" Yes, in context he is reading. A low score on nonsense words paired with a high score on real words in sentences is a huge red flag. It signals a potential issue when the student has to figure out unknown words by using knowledge of a word pattern. Teachers can't observe *how* students figure out words they don't know. It's impossible to know which words are familiar and which ones are not yet recognized. Some kids are really good at using context clues.

Learning new words by using context clues is a *good* skill but it's not the *best* skill. Teachers need to make sure students don't get by because they're really good at using only context clues in reading. Students need more ways to figure out words because at some point the process of either memorizing words or using context clues will fail them. A 1st grader can appear to be a good reader and then hit the wall in about 3rd or 4th grade. Have you seen discouraged 4th graders? It's not fun to build their confidence back up when they thought they were good readers in earlier grades and all of a sudden they are falling behind and can't figure out why. Because their gaps can go way back to 1st grade, it's harder to catch them up the later the problem is identified.

Using nonsense words for assessment can be a lightning rod for controversy. Often during workshops or coaching sessions, tempers rise and passionate discussions erupt about why we're even showing students nonsense words. Here's the rationale for using them: When a student reads a real word, teachers can't peek into his brain to see how he's reading the word. When nonsense words are presented, teachers can discover what the student knows about phonics patterns. Computer-administered assessments also can't do this. For diagnostic testing, it's critical to listen to the student's pronunciation of a nonsense word. Until voice recognition is perfect, a computer can't do this. These data are needed to place children in the right groups. If nonsense words are necessary to make sure we identify children early and they don't slip through until 4th grade, then we need to let go of our adult concerns and do what's right for children.

An Example of a Phonics Diagnostic Assessment

Let's look at an example of a student scoring form from a phonics diagnostic assessment. In the earlier example with 2nd graders Jose and Mary, the universal screener data indicated that the next step for Mary was a phonics diagnostic assessment. Because she's at the beginning of 2nd grade, her teacher will want to assess her on each of the key phonics skills that 1st graders are expected to master. This means that Mary's teacher should assess her on the following four skills: *consonant-vowel-consonant*, *consonant blend*, *consonant digraph*, and *long vowel silent*-e. In the *PSI*, these are known as Skills 2 through 5.

Imagine that Mary scores 90 percent on Skill 2 (*consonant-vowel-consonant*). Next, her teacher administers Skill 3 (*consonant blends*). Looking at Mary's scoring form, which appears in Figure 2.2, notice that her score on the nonsense portion is 5 correct out of 10, and she got 7 correct out of 10 on real words in sentences. A score of 90 percent or higher is necessary on the nonsense word to "pass," so Mary should be placed in the phonics group that will start working on words with short-vowel patterns including consonant blends.

FIGURE 2.2
Example of a Scoring Form for Consonant Blends

Skill 3: Consonant Blends (Error on blend and vowel)	
triz, ~~flug~~ *vug*, ~~blet~~ *plit*, mond, gamp ~~strom~~ *stom*, ~~splet~~ *spit*, prant, brund, ~~grest~~ *prest*	# Correct 5/10
~~Fred~~ *Ferd* was glad to swim to the raft at camp. Brad held on to the ~~strap~~ *storp* so he ~~could~~ *can't* jump off the ~~stilts~~ *splits*. (Error on sight word)	# Target Words Correct 7/10

Source: From 95 Percent Group Inc., *Phonics Screener for Intervention*™ (*PSI*™). Copyright © 95 Percent Group Inc. All rights reserved. Reprinted with permission.

Phonological Awareness Diagnostic Assessments

Diagnostic assessments for phonological awareness share the same purpose and administration features as phonics diagnostics. The only difference is that, because they assess a skill that is oral only, the student doesn't view text pages during assessment. For some skills, shapes and pictures are used to help reduce the memory load and get a more accurate view of the student's phonological awareness.

As with phonics assessments, assessing skills in order from simplest to most complex is recommended. The three major areas of phonological awareness are syllables, onset-rimes, and phonemes, in that order. The *Phonological Awareness Screener for Intervention* (*PASI*) from 95 Percent Group assesses a total of 25 subskills under those three areas, as follows:

- Syllable level—8 skills
- Onset-rime level—6 skills
- Phoneme level—11 skills

The process is similar to the process for phonics in that the universal screener provides enough information to identify students who appear to have a phonological awareness deficit. Most universal screeners assess one or two PA skills in kindergarten and 1st grade. Universal screeners typically assess the ability to identify enough first sounds in spoken words in a minute; this ability is called either Initial Sound Fluency or First Sound Fluency. If the assessor says the word *ball*, the correct student response is /b/. The second PA skill commonly assessed is phoneme segmentation, which is the ability to pull apart all the sounds in a spoken word. When the assessor says the word *mom*, the correct student response is /m/ /o/ /m/.

Figure 2.3 shows an example of a scoring form for phoneme segmentation in the *Phonological Awareness Screener for Intervention*. Notice that this student correctly segmented the two sounds in the word *my* and scored one point for that word. Yet he didn't get a point for any other word. To earn a point, the student must properly segment all the sounds in the word. On the second word, *map*, the student segmented the first sound, /m/, but then clustered the second and third sounds together as /ap/ instead of separating them as /a/ and /p/. Because the student got only one of five points on this skill, he would be

FIGURE 2.3
Student Scoring Form for Phonological Awareness Skill

		Directions: We're going to say every sound in a word. Listen: the word is *see*. The sounds in *see* are /s/ /ē/. Let's say every sound in more words.				
Skill 5.7	**Segmentation**	Say: my. Say each sound.	/m/ /ī/	/m/ /i/	1/1	**Kindergarten**
		Say: map. Say each sound.	/m/ /ă/ /p/	/m/ /ap/	0/1	
		Say: sock. Say each sound.	/s/ /ŏ/ /k/	/s/ /ock/	0/1	
		Say: flat. Say each sound.	/f/ /l/ /ă/ /t/	/f/ /lat/	0/1	
		Say: best. Say each sound.	/b/ /ĕ/ /s/ /t/	/bĕ/ /ĕst/	0/1	
STOP		If all correct, continue. Otherwise stop and assess with Long Form A, starting at Skill 5.5.		Score:	1/5	

placed in a group to begin working on phoneme segmentation, which is called Skill 5.7 in the *PASI*.

Forming Tier 2 and Tier 3 Groups with Diagnostic Data

After administering a diagnostic measure for all the students who are deficient in one of the areas, teachers need a way to cluster students who have similar deficits. A grouping worksheet with student names down the left side and skills listed in columns across the top will fill the need. The simplest way to make a grouping worksheet is to create it in a digital spreadsheet.

An example of a grouping worksheet for the *PSI* phonics diagnostic assessment is shown in Figure 2.4. Notice that there are two scores in each cell. The one on the left is the student's score on the "nonsense word" portion, and the one on the right is the score on the "real words in sentences." For example, Brian's data appear in the first row. On Skill 2 (*consonant-vowel-consonant*), he got 10 on both parts, and on Skill 3 (*consonant blends*), he got 7 correct in nonsense words and 10 on real words in sentences. The most important score for grouping is the nonsense word score. Because Brian needs a score of 9 or above to

FIGURE 2.4
Example of a Grouping Worksheet for Phonics Groups

Classroom Grouping Worksheet
(Basic and Advanced Phonics Skills and Sight Words)

Student Name	Form			Beginning Phonics Skills				Advanced Phonics Skills				Other
		1a: Letter Names	1b-1c: Letter Sounds	2: VC and CVC	3: Consonant Blends	4: Consonant Digraphs	5: Long Vowel Silent-e	6: Predictable Vowel Teams	7: Unpredictable Vowel Teams	8: Vowel-r	9: Complex Consonants	Sight Words
Points possible (pseudowords-real words)	A, B, C	26-n/a	21C 5V	10-10	10-10	10-10	10-10	10-10	10-10	10-10	10-10	n/a-220
Brian				10-10	7-10	7-10	2-10					
Hadley				10-10	7-4							
Becca				6-10	7-7	6-7						
Alyssa				10-10	9-9	9-10	7-7					
Mercedes				9-9	9-10	7-8	8-10					
Kristi				10-10	9-10	8-7	7-10					
Quinn				9-9	9-9	7-9	6-8					
Jeff				9-10	9-7	6-8	7-6					
Jordan				9-9	9-10	9-10	4-10					
Brittany				9-10	10-10	9-9	1-8					
Summer				10-10	9-10	10-9	6-10					
Shandra				9-10	10-10	9-9	7-9					
Jaden				9-10	10-10	9-10	7-8					

Source: From 95 Percent Group Inc., *Phonics Screener for Intervention™* (*PSI*™). Copyright © 95 Percent Group Inc. All rights reserved. Reprinted with permission.

indicate mastery, his intervention instruction should start with Skill 3. He also didn't pass Skills 4 and 5, but a student's intervention instruction always starts with the lowest missing skill.

The students are placed in three groups, indicating their starting point for intervention, as follows:

- Skill 3—Consonant Blends: Brian, Hadley, and Becca
- Skill 4—Consonant Digraphs: Mercedes, Kristi, Quinn, and Jeff
- Skill 5—Long Vowel Silent-*e*: Alyssa, Jordan, Brittany, Summer, Shandra, and Jaden

One critical point is that scores from the two parts of the phonics diagnostic should not be added together. Doing so masks important information. For example, if a student scores 8 on the nonsense word part and 10 on real words in sentences, adding the scores together would total 18 out of 20. This would meet the 90 percent benchmark threshold but mask the fact that the student doesn't use the pattern well enough with unfamiliar words. Using a combined score could lead to incorrect conclusions about whether a student can apply phonics knowledge to figure out unknown words as the text gets increasingly more difficult in later grades. Consider the score on real words in sentences as information. If in doubt, place a student in an intervention group for a few days, and if he shows mastery, pull him out of the group.

Notice that the group names align to the phonics skill names. Instead of having "Yellow Groups," "Strategic Groups," or "Below Benchmark Groups," the groups will be called "Consonant Blend Group" or "Long Vowel Silent-*e* Group."

Just like with phonics, once all students who are deficient in phonological awareness have been given the *PASI*, their teachers can enter their scores on a grouping worksheet like the one shown in Figure 2.5. As the figure indicates, two groups can be formed. Nicolas and Mia can be placed together, and they will start on the phoneme skill of *initial sound isolation* (which is the first phonemic awareness skill). The second group can be composed of Isabella, Jayden, and Lateeya, who need to work on *phoneme segmentation*, which is a skill about halfway up the series of skills at the phoneme level.

Seven Characteristics of a Good Diagnostic Assessment

How can schools distinguish a good diagnostic assessment from one that is less effective? They should look for seven characteristics, as described in the next paragraphs.

1. Breakout of subskills. Effective diagnostic assessments break out individual subskills. It's preferable for the assessor to measure one thing at a time rather than measuring several skills with a single word prompt. Although it

FIGURE 2.5

Example of a Grouping Worksheet for Phonological Awareness Groups

Skill 5: Phonemes

Student Name	Skill 5.1a Isolation (Initial Phoneme)	Skill 5.1b Isolation (Final Phoneme)	Skill 5.2 Application: Identification (Initial Phonemes)	Skill 5.3 Application: Categorization (Initial Phoneme)	Skill 5.4a Application: Categorization (Exclusion–3 Words)	Skill 5.4b Application: Categorization (Exclusion–4 Words)	Skill 5.5 Blending (2- and 3-Phoneme Words)	Skill 5.6 Segmentation (2- and 3-Phoneme Words)	Skill 5.7 Segmentation (4-Phoneme Words)	Skill 5.8 Application: Categorization (Number)	Skill 5.9a Manipulation: Addition (Initial)	Skill 5.9b Manipulation: Addition (Final)	Skill 5.10a Manipulation: Deletion (Initial)	Skill 5.10b Manipulation: Deletion (Final)	Skill 5.11a Manipulation: Substitution (Initial)	Skill 5.11b Manipulation: Substitution (Final)	Skill 5.11c Manipulation: Substitution (Medial)
Points Possible	5	5	5	5	5	5	5	5	5	5	5	5	5	5	5	5	5
Brittany Ortiz	5	5	5	5	5	5	5	5	5	5	5	5	5	5	5	5	5
Nicolas Garcia	4	2	4	3	3												
Harry Cho							5	5	5	5	5	5	5	3	4	2	0
Samuel Martinez																	
Lucas Torres																	
Sofia Roman								3									
Isabella Reyes							5		0								
Sara Masters																	
Tomas Ortiz	5	5	4	4	4	4	5	5	4	4	5	4	5	4	4	2	0
Jayden Gordon	5	5	4	4	4	4	4	0	0								
Lateeya Phillip	5	5	5	4	4	4	4	3	0								
Martin Diaz							5	5	3	2							
Angel Munoz																	
Mia Ortega	4	2	2														
Juliana Salazar																	
Kianna Lewis																	
Gabriel Medina							5	5	4	4	5	3	2				
Camila Ruiz							5	5	5	5	5	5	5	5	5	0	0

might seem that it would be more efficient if each word included several patterns, my experience is that this makes it harder for teachers to score and interpret results. Instead, it's preferable for an assessment to have one set of consonant-vowel-consonant words, for example, and another set of words with the long vowel silent-*e*.

2. Assessment of skills in order of complexity. Skills should be ordered so that the simplest ones are measured first, then the next difficult, and so on, up to the most complex. To do this, the assessment developers would need to start by developing a continuum that reflects the order of skill acquisition. The assessment should be aligned with research findings and the skill order of most state standards. Arranging skills in an order from simplest to most complex is essential for a shorter administration time. When the student fails to score a passing level on a skill, the assessment can stop. The diagnosis is a discovery process to figure out how far up the continuum the student is in terms of mastering skills. At the point where the student can't pass any more skills, the assessor stops testing—that's where intervention should begin.

3. Separate indicator scores. Subskill data from a diagnostic assessment should not be added together to reach a composite score. For example, a phonics diagnostic assessment would have one score for CVC, another one for consonant blends, and a different score for short vowels with blends. Adding all the scores together doesn't achieve the purpose, which is to pinpoint what the student needs and where to start instruction. A composite benchmark score is meaningless because it might simply verify that a student has a phonics deficit but fail to pinpoint the lowest missing skill for group placement.

4. At least two alternate forms. Because diagnostic assessments are often the best tool for progress monitoring, it's critical to select one that has at least two alternate forms. An alternate form is a duplicate of the initial form, with the same skills, type of scoring sheet, and instructions. The only thing that changes is the probes; that is, the words students are asked to read are different than the ones they read when initially assessed.

Typical practice is to have three forms, and sometimes even more. When there are three forms, they are used in the following manner:

- Form A—initial assessment and first group placement
- Form B—first round of progress monitoring to see if instruction has worked and whether the student is ready to be moved up to a higher group

• Form C—rarely used (only if a child spends another cycle in the same skill group); need fresh probes to see if the student has made progress or mastered it

It's important to monitor progress with an alternate form. The timing between assessments is short, and if teachers don't use different probes, students could remember the words from the first time they saw them only a few weeks earlier.

5. Clarity on which skills to administer by grade level. Because diagnostic assessments are designed to measure mastery of an area of skill, they do not have separate versions by grade level. The skills start at the lowest level and take a stepping-stone path up to the top skill. Teachers need to know when to stop administering based on expected skill mastery at various grade levels. For example, the phonological awareness diagnostic is designed with a progression of skills to be mastered during kindergarten. Up through January, students should be mastering the syllable and onset-rime skills; after January the phoneme-level skills are evaluated. Students who have mastered all these skills by the end of the year have met the expectations for kindergarten.

6. Short administration time. An effective diagnostic assessment takes a short time to administer. It's possible to get enough information on phonics concepts with 10 nonsense-word probes per skill, which takes less than a minute per skill to assess. The amount of time it takes to test a student depends upon how well she does; testing continues until the student fails a skill. Sometimes it's recommended to go up one skill after the student fails to make sure she doesn't pass that next skill on the continuum. In this case, assess one more skill to discover if the failure on a single skill is a gap that can be addressed quickly before placing her in a higher group.

7. No need to administer *all* skills at a given time. The best diagnostic assessments are designed so that it's not necessary to give the entire test at once. Once a student fails a skill, it is a waste of the teacher's and the student's time to finish the entire diagnostic assessment. Because the skills are in order of difficulty, once a student fails a skill, it's very unlikely that he'll pass the skills above that one. The student is placed in a group to receive intervention in the lowest missing skill.

After a reasonable period of intervention (typically a couple of weeks of 30 minutes of daily intervention), the teacher gives an alternate form to monitor progress. If the student passes that skill, then testing continues up the skill sequence until he fails again, whether that occurs at the very next skill or one a bit further up the continuum.

Summing Up

Diagnostic assessments are critical tools in implementing MTSS. Without them, it's unlikely that teachers will have the data needed to uncover which skills have been mastered and which are deficient. Students can only be placed in tight skill groups when teachers can pinpoint the lowest missing skill on a continuum. Diagnostic assessments work in concert with universal screeners. The universal screener identifies *who* is below benchmark, and the diagnostic assessment tells *why* the student is not at benchmark and points to where to start intervention for most efficient use of Tier 2 and Tier 3 instructional time.

Although giving a phonological awareness or phonics diagnostic to every student isn't recommended, it's surprising how many teachers do it anyway after using these assessments with their struggling readers. Today there is a lot of conversation about teachers believing too much time is spent on assessments. So why would they elect to assess when it's not recommended? It appears that the information is valuable enough that it's worth the time to get the data for all their students.

Why are so many schools not using diagnostic assessments, given that they are inexpensive and are an important cog in the wheel of MTSS? It's likely that schools not using diagnostic assessments simply don't know about them, don't understand the different types of assessments, or don't realize that this kind of data isn't available from other tests they are already giving.

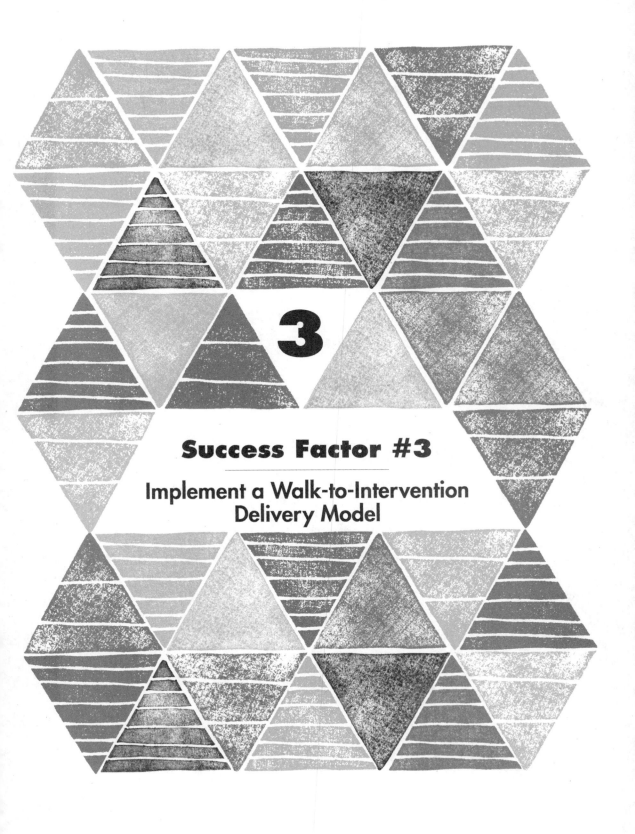

3

Success Factor #3

Implement a Walk-to-Intervention
Delivery Model

The third success factor for implementation of MTSS concerns how schools organize to deliver small-group interventions in Tiers 2 and 3. As described in the previous chapters, the first two success factors are about pinpointing students' key deficit skills and using data from a universal screener and a diagnostic assessment to place students in tight skill groups. Now that students are placed, how will teachers organize to teach those small groups?

MTSS involves much more than assessing, analyzing data, and placing students in groups based on skill deficits. It's also about how educators implement structures to provide small-group intervention to the right kids, in the right group, receiving the appropriate differentiated instruction, and moving them between groups until they catch up to benchmark. The model a school chooses for how to deliver intervention in small groups influences how robust its gains will be.

In this chapter, we'll explore two different models and compare the advantages of one over the other. These two particular models were selected because they represent the most common ones schools use, and they provide a contrast that enables analyzing the strengths and weaknesses of alternative approaches.

Model 1—In-Class Intervention

In Model 1, every student stays in his or her homeroom during intervention time, and two groups are meeting while the other students are working independently. Imagine a classroom teacher working on a particular skill with the first group at a kidney-shaped table in a corner, and another instructor in another area of the classroom working on a different skill with a second group. Each of the two groups has four or five students working with the teacher or another instructor.

Let's assume that each intervention group has five students. That's a total of 10 students working with the two instructors. Where are the rest of the 15 students in the class? They are at work stations or at their desks doing independent work. Common stations might include a writing station, a computer listening station, and a quiet reading corner. What are these 15 other students doing during intervention time? The answer is, whatever they want. Some of them may be fully engaged in productive work during those 30 minutes. Yet it's likely that some are not making good use of that independent time.

This model offers some advantages. One advantage is that there is no loss of time related to students having to move outside their classroom. Remaining with their classroom teacher also means that the students are familiar with classroom management practices. Scheduling is easier—there's no need to coordinate intervention with the other classrooms at a particular grade level because students aren't mixed with those in other classes. The homeroom teacher will have complete information about what each student is working on during intervention time, and she can carry instructional techniques back and forth between Tier 1 and intervention.

Model 2—Walk-to-Intervention

Model 2 is an approach that our consultants call the "Walk-to-Intervention" delivery model, because students walk to the location of their intervention group, which may not be in their homeroom classroom. The entire grade-level team must have intervention scheduled at a common time because students are assigned to a group based on specific need regardless of their homeroom. If their assigned group is not taught by their homeroom teacher, students move to another classroom nearby or perhaps to a common area where a group is meeting.

Schools implementing this model call it many different things. One of the most common names is "WIN" time, which stands for "What I Need." Another common practice is to name it after the school mascot, like "Cougar Time," "Leopard Time," or "Mustang Time."

Let's look at some numbers. Imagine that there are 94 3rd graders in four classrooms. Third grade has a daily 30-minute intervention block from 10:30 to 11:00 a.m., during which all four classroom teachers will teach intervention groups. In addition to classroom teachers, the principal has scheduled two other staff members to teach 3rd grade groups during that intervention block. The teachers have met, analyzed all the student data, and placed the 3rd graders into the following six intervention groups:

- Group 1: Enrichment group (30 students)—Students are reading and writing above-benchmark text.
- Group 2: Fluency group (30 students)—Following short modeling by the teacher, students are paired to read to their partner, who scores words read correctly.
- Group 3: Advanced Word Study group (18 students)—Students are working on routines to use one of the six syllable types to read unknown multisyllable words more efficiently.
- Group 4: *R*-Control Vowel group (6 students)—Students are receiving explicit instruction on how to read words that contain *r*-control vowels (*-ar, -or, -er, -ir*, and *-ur*).
- Group 5: Vowel Team group (5 students)—Students are working on reading words that contain vowel team patterns (*-ee, -igh, -ai/-ay, -oi/-oy*, etc.).
- Group 6: Long Vowel Silent-*e* group (5 students)—Students are receiving explicit instruction on reading words with the long vowel sound with the silent-*e* spelling (*-ake, -ate, -ike*, etc.).

Notice the specificity of the skill groups. The diagnostic assessment reveals a student's lowest missing skill, and because there are six groups, each student is placed in a group to receive instruction in a very specific skill. Students who can read the words but aren't fluent are in a group working on that skill; they are almost at benchmark. The students who are in the Advanced Word Study group read single-syllable words well but are struggling with multisyllable words. The three other groups are even further below 3rd grade expectations, which is why their groups are the smallest. Long vowel silent-*e* is a phonics pattern that is generally mastered by 1st grade, according to standards. These six groups provide a way for teachers to offer differentiated instruction to each of the 94 3rd graders.

Advantages of the Walk-to-Intervention Model

The schools that are getting the best results are using the Walk-to-Intervention model. The reason for these strong results is related to the 10 advantages described here.

1. Multiple specific skill groups are taught at the same time. In the 3rd grade example just described, Model 1 has two groups and Model 2 has six groups. With only two groups, how can a classroom teacher provide all students what they need? Some teachers using Model 1 split the time slot in half so all below-benchmark students participate in one of the teacher's groups for 15 of the 30 minutes. Four groups will meet, but the struggling readers get only half as much teacher-directed explicit instruction in the skill they need to close the gap.

2. Every group has an instructor. In Model 1, the students not participating in one of the two teacher-led intervention groups are on their own during intervention time. It's difficult to ensure that students working independently are fully utilizing the time. Having a teacher instructing each group, as in Model 2, assures the principal that all students are getting explicit teacher-directed instruction during the intervention block. Model 1 generally leads to a lot of interruptions because one of the two instructors has to stop to ask for quiet or to answer individual questions. Even the best classroom management practices won't avoid some interruptions to help the students engaging in the unsupervised activities.

For schools that use guided reading groups during Tier 1 core curriculum time, the Walk-to-Intervention advantage of having an instructor teaching each group is an especially important attribute. Students are already expected to be engaged in productive activities during the time the teacher is meeting with other guided reading groups.

One comment often heard from schools implementing this model is that it enables differentiation for *all* students—not just the struggling readers. Because the benchmark students are spending time with a teacher working with above-benchmark text, there is less risk that they will not be offered the opportunity to excel and reach the levels they should achieve.

> Too frequently the teachers' paradigm is that they send students *out* of their class for intervention. Somebody else teaches "those kids."

3. All classroom teachers are teaching small groups during intervention time. Most veteran elementary teachers report spending some of their career in schools where the culture encourages a belief that struggling readers are the responsibility of the reading specialists, Title I teachers, or instructional aides. Too frequently the teachers' paradigm is that they send students *out* of their class for intervention. Somebody else teaches "those kids." In the Walk-to-Intervention model, all the classroom teachers are teaching groups during the intervention block, so they are an integral part of differentiation for students.

4. Less extra help is required. In the context of the example with the four classes of 3rd graders, Model 1 uses four extra instructors versus two extra instructors for Model 2, because in the first instance an assistant comes into each classroom during intervention time.

5. Group sizes are varied based on need. As seen in the 3rd grade example, the size of the skill groups varies a lot. The groups that are at or closest to benchmark are the largest. The benchmark and fluency groups are the very largest, with 30 students each. The next group, with 18, is for students who are fluent reading one-syllable words but stumble reading multisyllable words. The other three groups are the smallest, with five or six students who are furthest behind on skills. If a seventh instructor is available, then a comprehension group could be formed by pulling some students from the top two groups. Alternatively, that seventh person might enable the 16 students in the lowest three groups to be split into four groups.

6. Any grade level—even kindergarten—can use this model. While working with a Florida district about a dozen years ago, my advice was to start the Walk-to-Intervention model with grades 1 and above. After all, I thought, kindergartners are so young, and they wouldn't do well traveling outside their own familiar classroom and being with a different teacher for small-group time. The transition time would make this model ineffective. It would be chaos, right?

During a return coaching visit a few months later, the kindergarten team sheepishly "confessed" that they had implemented a Walk-to-Intervention model and they invited me to observe it in action. That was a defining moment in my work. This dedicated team had developed some helpful transition strategies, like giving each student a lanyard with one of six animals on it. At the start of the intervention block, the kindergarten classroom doors opened and the students filed out to spot the teacher holding a sign with their animal on it. No big deal. The students transitioned easily, and throughout the day they enthusiastically greeted other teachers in the hallway. I offer only one piece of advice: don't start this model during the first month of kindergarten. Give these 5-year-olds a brief period to adjust to school.

7. Collaboration among grade-level colleagues is encouraged. When teachers work day in and day out with a struggling reader, it can be hard to keep trying to figure out what to do next. Teachers can feel like they've exhausted their toolkit. They've tried everything they know how to do for that student, and he's still not making progress in learning to read. An advantage of the Walk-to-Intervention model is that a grade-level colleague will be teaching that student in her intervention group during the intervention block, so she's also had a chance to observe that student's struggles. Not only is it reassuring that the student is getting the benefit of a different approach or perspective, but the teachers also benefit from having someone to talk with about which instructional strategies seem to be most effective with that student. When the team's goal is to get all grade-level students to benchmark, it's reassuring for teachers to have an attitude of "we're all in this together" and not feel they're on their own.

8. Struggling readers are not singled out. Students who receive special services or extra support are typically pulled out of the classroom to work with a support teacher. They leave at various times throughout the day and are missing out on the whole-class instruction for that period. How do teachers even keep track of what they were teaching when each student left the room? It has to be challenging figuring out what every child who left the room missed, let alone finding the time to work with each student later.

In the Walk-to-Intervention model, every student goes to a group during the 30-minute intervention block (even those at and above benchmark). Therefore, the below-benchmark students aren't missing another activity during intervention time; there isn't more work to make up for what they missed.

There's another important reason this model is preferable. The below-benchmark students don't feel singled out and conscious of needing special help. It's not as obvious who is below benchmark when everyone goes to a group during the 30-minute block.

9. Teachers can specialize in what they teach during intervention time. Because there are many different skill groups taught at the same time, teachers can gravitate toward a skill that they enjoy teaching. Some teachers like teaching comprehension or fluency more than decoding, whereas other teachers are really knowledgeable about phonics. The Walk-to-Intervention model is well suited to specialization, with teachers selecting which skill area they want to teach. This approach also gives students the benefit of working with a teacher who is proficient and enthusiastic about the exact area they need.

One of the most challenging aspects of getting this model started can be hesitation or resistance. If there's resistance, it will come from the teachers and not the students. Students love it! They like knowing other teachers in the building and mixing with kids outside their classroom. Sometimes a teacher doesn't believe that her grade-level colleagues are as good at reading instruction as she is. Whether that's true or not doesn't matter. Total teacher participation is necessary for this to work. One way to address this issue is to encourage the less skilled teacher to elect to teach something other than her weak area.

> After the model has been in place for a while, principals will say, "My teachers are saying 'our kids' instead of 'my kids.'" What an amazing paradigm shift.

10. An unintended positive consequence emerges in the form of "our kids." Over the many years that we've been guiding schools to use the Walk-to-Intervention model, we've heard one comment over and over again. After the model has been in place for a while, principals will say something like, "My teachers are saying 'our kids' instead of 'my kids.'" What an amazing paradigm shift—and an unintended positive consequence. It's not the reason a school should adopt the Walk-to-Intervention model; the reason to do it is because students' reading improves more with this model than with other approaches. Yet it's truly satisfying to have teachers share responsibility for getting an entire grade level of "our" students to benchmark.

Getting Started with Intervention Groups

Once schools have decided that they want to implement a Walk-to-Intervention model, the next consideration is how to get started. Here are the steps to successful implementation.

Step 1: Collect All Data Needed for Grouping

As discussed in Chapter 2, administering a universal screener to all students is the first step. The universal screener data help identify the students who score at the below-benchmark level and will need a diagnostic evaluation. Looking at the benchmark levels on the individual indicators of the universal assessment leads to selecting the appropriate diagnostic assessment. The composite score signals which children need help; because it's a weighted average of several indicators, this is when looking at the scores on all indicators is critical. Once each struggling reader has been assessed with either a phonological awareness or a phonics diagnostic assessment, as appropriate, the team is ready to determine the first groups of the year.

Step 2: Form Initial Groups

Placing students in initial groups requires the participation of the entire grade-level team. The goal is to place each student in his or her optimum group. The process involves figuring out the most immediate skill deficit for each student, considering the number of staff members available to teach groups, and then deciding the best way to meet all students' needs with the staff available. It's like a lot of things in life—there's never enough. In this case, there is never enough staff to have very small groups for every skill. Therefore, it's a process of balancing to ensure that all students are placed so that their needs are met while ensuring that the groups that are the furthest behind receive the most intensive intervention by placement in the smallest groups.

For grade-level teams forming groups for the first time, the best process to follow is to use sticky notes and a whiteboard. Typically, a reading coach or an administrator will assist with this initial effort. It's advisable to schedule this meeting about one week after the close of the benchmark assessment window. For example, if the two-week fall benchmark window is September 11–22, then collection of the diagnostic data needs to be completed during the week of September 25–29. Schedule the grouping meeting for September 29.

Grade-level teachers will need to do some preparation before the meeting. The diagnostic data pinpoint the lowest missing skill on a continuum, which is the student's starting point. Teachers prepare a sticky note with the student's name and skill. The reading coach or an administrator will have written column labels for the various skills on a whiteboard in the meeting room. Teachers arrive at the meeting with a stack of sticky notes and put each one under the relevant skill column on the whiteboard. (Sometimes schools give each teacher a different color of sticky note so they can easily locate their students on the board.)

Once all the sticky notes are up on the whiteboard, everyone can see the number of students across the grade level needing help in the various skill areas. Before the meeting, the principal needs to have determined the number of additional staff members who will be scheduled to teach during intervention block time. Going back to the 3rd grade example described earlier in this chapter, there were four classroom teachers and two additional staff members, for a total of six instructors for the 94 students.

Step 3: Balance Group Size and Number of Staff Members

The team now must move the sticky notes into six clusters. It's easiest to look at the top and bottom first. The benchmark group is the first one to examine. If the group is not too large for one instructor, then that group is formed. The teachers should move next to the students with the lowest missing skills who need the smallest groups. Typically, there are two groups at the lowest end. So far, three of the six groups have been formed. Then the teachers look at all the students in the middle. Balancing the group size for the students in the middle is the greatest challenge. If a seventh instructor can be identified, assigning the rest of the groups is easier. Figure 3.1 shows an example of typical groups for the beginning of the year for 1st and 3rd grade with six groups.

FIGURE 3.1
Groups for 1st Grade and 3rd Grade, First Half of the Year

1st Grade			3rd Grade		
Phonological Awareness			**Phonological Awareness**		
Phoneme	Isolation	X			
	Segmentation and blending	X			
	Manipulation	X			
Phonics			**Phonics**		
Short Vowel	CVC	X	Short Vowel	CVC, blends, and digraphs	X
	Consonant blends				
	Consonant digraphs	X			
Long Vowel			Long Vowel	Long vowel silent-e	X
Vowel Teams			Vowel Teams	Vowel teams–simple	X
				Vowel teams–complex	X
Consonant Clusters					
Multisyllable Words				Closed and long vowel silent-e syllables	X
Other			**Other**		
Fluency			Fluency		
Comprehension			Comprehension		
Benchmark		X	Benchmark		X

Source: From 95 Percent Group Inc. Copyright © 95 Percent Group Inc. Used with permission.

Later Adjustments to the Grouping Process

After the initial grouping, the process gets easier. As described in the next paragraphs, progress monitoring can lead to some students moving from one group to another, and schools can use a less complicated process for tracking students' placement.

Moving Students After Collecting Progress-Monitoring Data

Imagine that the intervention groups have met for a few weeks. Teachers administer a progress-monitoring assessment to see if the students have mastered the skill that was taught. Some students will be ready to exit the skill they've been studying, and they will be assigned to a different group to work on their next-lowest missing skill. Occasionally a student stays in place for an additional cycle because the progress-monitoring data show that the missing skill wasn't mastered with the first cycle of instruction.

Let's look at our 3rd grade example again. Assume that the movement between the first and second cycles occurred in the four lowest groups. The students in the two highest groups (the benchmark and fluency groups) remained in their groups for the second cycle. There are 34 students in Groups 3 through 6—where the movement occurred after the first round of intervention. Three students in Group 6 moved to Group 5, leaving only two students in the lowest group, who need a second round of instruction in the long vowel silent-*e* skill. The three participants in Group 6 who moved up advanced to either Group 3 or 4. Notice in Figure 3.2 that by the seventh cycle, there are still six groups, but the Group 6 skill is no longer needed, and so many students have moved up to benchmark that there are now two enrichment groups.

Switching to a Simpler Tracking System

The sticky-note process described earlier is really helpful the first couple of grouping cycles because it gives a visual presentation of the groups. It helps teachers see the tradeoffs between the size of the group and meeting all students' needs with the available staffing. Once the team understands that tradeoff, it is no longer necessary to see it in that way.

After about the third cycle of regrouping, most schools abandon the sticky-note process and instead use a spreadsheet that resides on the school server.

FIGURE 3.2
Number of Students in Each Group

Group	Cycle 1	Cycle 2	Cycle 7
1—Enrichment group	1 group—30 students	1 group—30 students	2 groups—60 students
2—Fluency group	1 group—30 students	1 group—30 students	1 group—10 students
3—Advanced word study group	1 group—18 students	1 group—20 students	1 group—16 students
4—R-control vowel group	1 group—6 students	1 group—6 students	1 group—6 students
5—Vowel-team group	1 group—5 students	1 group—6 students	1 group—2 students
6—Long vowel silent-e group	1 group—5 students	1 group—2 students	
Total Number of Students	94	94	94

Source: From 95 Percent Group Inc. Copyright © 95 Percent Group Inc. Used with permission.

Imagine that all intervention teachers upload progress-monitoring data for the students in their intervention group by the end of the day on Thursday. Then one person, typically the reading coach, reviews the data and determines the new groups. By Friday noon, each instructor checks the sheet on the server to see which skill she will be teaching the next week and the names of the students who are going to be in her new group. The teachers are now ready to pull the materials needed for instructing their new group, which starts on Monday.

When the implementation reaches this stage, it's no longer necessary to use a grade-level-team meeting for grouping. There's now time to talk about how well all the students are doing, to work out any issues, and to focus on figuring out what else to try with the students who aren't progressing.

Grouping Across Grade Levels

A question that occasionally is asked at MTSS workshops is whether grouping across grade levels is a good idea. This question rarely comes up at large schools but is a real issue for small schools. The difficulty for these schools is not having enough different groups for struggling readers to join.

The threshold size for grouping within a grade level seems to be three classroom teachers and two additional instructors, for a total of five groups.

Assuming the principal can assign other instructors to help the grade-level teachers, there are usually five or more groups, so teachers will have plenty of alternative groups to meet the needs of all their struggling readers. All the teachers will need to have a common intervention time for the Walk-to-Intervention model to work. Therefore, the schedule of assistants has to be aligned so they are assigned to teach intervention groups beside the grade-level classroom teachers. Scheduling the assistants is difficult enough without also trying to group across grade levels.

Grouping across grade levels is necessary in very small schools with only one or two teachers per grade level. The solution is to cluster a couple of grade levels based on typical student needs. The best option is to schedule the intervention for kindergarten and grade 1 at the same time, grades 2 and 3 together, and so on. These clusters of grades tend to have more skills in common. This approach is not perfect, but teachers will have to work together to enable more possible groups so they have more options for placement.

Scheduling an Intervention Block

Schools that are getting the best results have added an intervention block to the school's master schedule. In some locations, "literacy" has a 120-minute block, and teachers are left to figure out when intervention takes place during the literacy block. This approach doesn't work for the Walk-to-Intervention model, which requires a common intervention block for the entire grade-level team. Even if a school is implementing Model 1, nothing should take priority over intervention and nothing should push it aside even if the day gets crazy. Consistency of daily intervention matters for student progress.

Resistance to the Walk-to-Intervention Model

As mentioned earlier, if there is going to be resistance to implementing the Walk-to-Intervention model, it is more likely to come from the teachers than the students. In our initial discussions with elementary-grade teachers, we often hear three reasons why they aren't sure they want to implement this approach. These reasons are related to accountability, time, and uncertainty about colleagues' ability.

1. Accountability. Teachers are concerned that students are not in their homeroom for a full period of the instructional day and yet they are held accountable for student achievement as reflected in assessment data. This concern is raised more in states, districts, and schools where a teacher's evaluation (and a portion of compensation) is linked to test scores.

2. Loss of time to transition to groups. Teachers sometimes raise concerns about the time that it will take for students to travel to and from their homeroom and the location of their intervention groups. Unlike teachers in the secondary grades, elementary teachers aren't accustomed to students getting core instruction from other teachers. They teach the core areas of literacy, math, science, and social studies to the students assigned to them all year.

3. Believing a colleague may not teach as well. This third reason is the most difficult one to address. Sometimes a teacher feels she is a better teacher than one or more of her grade-level colleagues. This belief may actually be true, and it's the really good teachers who struggle the most with it. In the MTSS/RTI framework, teachers see the data for the entire grade level; everyone knows whose students end the year with considerably larger gains than students in other homerooms.

There are several ways to address this challenge. K–2 teachers whose students excel in literacy tend to be viewed as masters at reading instruction. When a teacher resists the Walk-to-Intervention model for this reason, try asking this master teacher to instruct the lowest groups while her "less capable" peer is assigned the fluency or benchmark groups. Fluency is easier to teach because students are typically reading text to a peer, and benchmark students can flourish when they work with above-benchmark text and dedicate time to reading and writing in response to the text.

Regardless of which reason a teacher has for resisting the model, the key is to get the grade level to try it. If good results follow, those who were reluctant will come around. If the kids are doing well, then teachers will buy into the model even if they had reservations initially. Concerns about accountability, loss of teaching time, and trust in colleagues' instruction all go away once the data show that students are doing better than they did before this approach was implemented.

Occasionally it helps to get part of the grade-level team to try the Walk-to-Intervention model for a few weeks. Then their enthusiasm encourages others to come onboard. There's nothing like data to convince resisters. When the student data show the model is working, it's pretty hard to stonewall it. If the resistance persists, the principal has to get involved and talk it through until everyone is doing what the evidence shows is best for students.

Summing Up

Schools can choose between two alternate models for how to organize and deliver intervention groups. In Model 1, all students remain in their homerooms during the intervention block. A second instructor comes into the classroom and teaches a group at the same time that the teacher works with a different small group. The other students work independently at work stations. Model 2, the Walk-to-Intervention model, has students grouped across the entire grade level and moving to the location where their group is meeting, which may be outside their homeroom.

The Walk-to-Intervention model has 10 advantages, including the fact that students are all placed in an instructor-led group and thus each teacher has more skill groups available to meet the needs of each student. Group sizes vary, so students who are furthest behind are placed in the smallest groups. Teachers have to collaborate, and often a paradigm shift occurs as teachers begin to refer to "our students" across the grade level rather than "my students" in "my home-room." In addition, the grade-level team thinks and acts more systemically.

Success Factor #4

Monitor Progress with an
Appropriate Assessment

Within a school's MTSS framework, progress monitoring is a tool that is similar to a GPS system or device on a road trip. It's pretty much impossible to say that a school is implementing MTSS if it doesn't have an effective progress-monitoring process. There are two common problems associated with progress monitoring, however. Sometimes the wrong assessment instruments are given, so the data aren't all that useful. In other situations, the amount of time set aside for teachers to use the data for making interim decisions is inadequate.

Let's start with a caution about this topic. Your state or district may have guidelines about what is expected for progress monitoring, and they might differ from the guidelines offered in this book. Of course, state and district guidelines must supersede what's advised here.

The Purpose of Progress Monitoring

Why is progress monitoring critical in MTSS? Progress-monitoring data are what inform decisions between benchmark periods about moving students in and out of groups. The information especially helps teachers decide when to exit a student from his current group and which skill the student needs next. The initial group placement is determined based on data from the universal screener and the results from the first time the student is tested with the diagnostic assessment. Most schools schedule their beginning-of-year (BOY) testing window about two to three weeks into the school year. Therefore, by early to mid-September—depending on when the school year starts—most schools have completed BOY testing. The resulting data are used to form initial intervention groups.

After the initial groups have met for a certain amount of time, the next step is to see how the interventions are working. That's the role of the progress-monitoring assessment. Without progress-monitoring data, teachers would have to guess or wait until after the next benchmark window to move students to new groups, which is too long. If students are moved only after benchmark assessments, they will have stayed in the same group for 12 to 15 weeks. Students should be moving in and out of intervention groups fluidly; if they master the skill in, say, three weeks, they should move to the group working on the next-lowest missing skill.

This chapter addresses two common issues related to how schools approach progress monitoring: (1) use of the wrong measure for progress monitoring and (2) failure to effectively use the progress-monitoring data to move students between groups.

Choosing the Correct Assessment Measure

One key to effective progress monitoring is to select an instrument that specifically measures the target skill. The best choice is an assessment that will tell the teacher if the student learned what was just taught in the intervention group. Too often there is a misalignment between the focus skill and what is being measured. This misalignment occurs when schools believe that all students' progress should be monitored with an alternate form of the universal screener. Although this approach is sometimes the best measure, that is not always the case. Let's look at a couple of examples.

If the focus of the skill group is fluency, then a good assessment for that is one that measures oral reading fluency. For a phonics group focused on vowel teams, an alternate form of the phonics diagnostic assessment is the best measure for that skill. Asking a student in the phonics group to read an oral reading fluency passage from the universal screener just isn't going to help because the passage doesn't have enough vowel-team words to indicate success or failure. Alternatively, when students read nonsense vowel-team syllables, the assessor can see if they are likely to be successful decoding that pattern in unknown real words. Best practice is to align the progress-monitoring measurement to the skill being taught. Quite often the best progress-monitoring instrument will be an alternate form of a phonological awareness or phonics diagnostic assessment.

Is it worthwhile to periodically reassess with a universal screener? Yes, sometimes. It depends upon how far below grade level the student is reading. If the student is in a skill group that is close to grade-level expectations, giving the universal screener one time between benchmark time periods is useful. If the student is way behind, then progress monitoring with the universal screener just continues to show that the student is well below benchmark, a determination that is already known.

Effective Use of Data

Progress-monitoring data not only provide information about individual students but also give information for other purposes. One important purpose of MTSS data is to see how well an entire grade level is doing at getting all students to reach or exceed benchmark. One way to do this is to have each grade-level team create a pyramid at the beginning of the year showing the percent of students in the three tiers: At or Above Benchmark, Below Benchmark, and Well Below Benchmark. The team then establishes goals for the percent of students that they hope are at benchmark by the middle of the year and the end of the year.

It's motivating for the teams to see the student growth from the beginning to the end of the year as the percentages in each tier of the pyramid change, with the percentage of Well Below Benchmark students shrinking and the At or Above Benchmark level growing. Teachers are working hard at interventions, and there's nothing quite like seeing visible improvements in the pyramid. It's time to celebrate.

Another way to track improvements is through data walls. Some schools create data walls that enable the observation of individual as well as grade-level progress. One of my favorite approaches involves using sticky notes in colors with significant meanings. Teachers use a red sticky note for students who started the year at the Well Below Benchmark level, yellow for those Below Benchmark, and green for those At or Above Benchmark. They then display the notes on a chart with three sections: green at the top, yellow in the middle, and red at the bottom.

At the initial grouping, each sticky-note color matches the section color. All students whose initial benchmark level is red are posted in the red area. At each subsequent regrouping, the notes start to mix up against the background. Red notes move up to the yellow zone, and yellow notes move to the green area. If a green note drops to the yellow zone, it's time to look at what is causing that student to slip a level. When there's a red note in the green zone, the entire team celebrates that student's success.

One of the best reports—although, sadly, it's rarely used—is called an "effectiveness report." The report looks at the effectiveness of instruction for students in each benchmark area—red, yellow, and green. The purpose of the effectiveness report is to look at changes across time, and therefore it's calculated between two periods; the report can be run from BOY to MOY, BOY to EOY, or MOY to EOY. To remove the impact of mobility, students must be assessed in both periods or their data are not included. The report has three columns showing how well students who started the year at the same instructional level performed: At or Above Benchmark, Below Benchmark, and Well Below Benchmark. It shows whether students stayed at the same level, moved up one level, or moved up two levels to reach benchmark if they started at the Well Below level. The At or Above Benchmark column shows the percent still at benchmark, the percent that slipped one level, and the percent that slipped two levels (hopefully there are none). See Figure 4.1 for a table showing an example of an effectiveness report for kindergarten from the beginning of the year to the middle of the year.

Are the data in Figure 4.1 encouraging? Some news is good, and some suggests areas of challenge. First, let's compare the overall percentages in each of the three categories. There is improvement overall, as follows:

- The percentage of students at benchmark score level increased from 33 percent at the beginning of the year (BOY) to 69 percent at the middle of the year (MOY).
- The percentage of students at Below Benchmark score level decreased from 40 percent to 6 percent.

FIGURE 4.1
Percentages Indicating Kindergarten Effectiveness of Instruction, by Students' Level at Middle of Year

At Middle of Year (MOY)	Percentage of Students Who Were <u>Well Below Benchmark</u> at BOY 37%	Percentage of Students Who Were <u>Below Benchmark</u> at BOY 40%	Percentage of Students Who Were <u>At or Above Benchmark</u> at BOY 33%
At or Above Benchmark	13%	44%	74%
Below Benchmark	26%	44%	19%
Well Below Benchmark	61%	12%	7%
	38 of 138 students (27%)	9 of 138 students (6%)	95 of 138 students (69%)

• The percentage of students at Well Below Benchmark decreased from 37 percent to 27 percent.

Now let's figure out how students moved. It's crucial to see whether some moved down within the levels while others moved up. The far-right column shows that only about three-fourths (74 percent) of the students who started the year at benchmark remained at benchmark at the middle of the year. This indicates an instructional issue with the Tier 1 core curriculum, because these students are not receiving Tier 2 or Tier 3 intervention. The core curriculum is not supporting approximately one-fourth of the students in making enough progress to reach the progressively higher expectations of the benchmark level as the year progresses.

Now let's look at the column for students who started the year Below Benchmark (often identified in the yellow zone). Forty-four percent of them moved up to benchmark in three months, which signals that the intervention groups are working. This is good news, and the year is only half over. Twelve percent dropped a level; this percentage equals one student, because there are only nine students in this category.

The greatest challenges of intervention are in moving the lowest students up. The Well Below Benchmark column shows that nearly 40 percent of this lowest group moved up either one level (26 percent) or two levels (13 percent). This upward movement is good. If the grade-level team double-dips to get more intervention time for these students, the rate of improvement may even increase. As more students enter the At or Above Benchmark group, the size of the lowest groups can be smaller, which also helps.

One of the most important things about this report is that mobility is not a factor because only the students who are assessed in both periods are included. Schools with high levels of mobility often find that their data are murky because students are moving in and out. They aren't present for more than one assessment, so comparisons from one assessment to the next are not possible for those students.

Once teachers have access to an effectiveness report, they can analyze the results guided by the following list of questions and answers:

Question: Which grade level is most effective at Tier 1?

Answer: The one that had the highest percentage of kids who entered the period At or Above Benchmark and are still at that level.

Question: Which grade level did the best at moving up Below Benchmark kids?

Answer: The one that moved the most students up a level to At or Above Benchmark and the fewest down a level to Below Benchmark.

Question: Which grade level did the best at moving up the Well Below Benchmark students?

Answer: The one that moved the most students up one level to Below Benchmark and two levels to At or Above Benchmark.

It's possible to look at an individual teacher's effectiveness compared to the effectiveness of the grade level as a whole. One of the best ways to convince a resistant teacher is to show her the effectiveness of her class versus the total effectiveness of the other classes at the grade level. If her students' scores haven't improved as much as the grade-level total, ask why she thinks that is so.

> When a school builds a reliable firewall at the lowest grades, fewer students will reach 4th grade reading at the Below Benchmark level.

Keep in mind that it's always harder to close the gap for higher grades than lower grades. Moving students up a level is easier with kindergarten students than it is with 4th graders. When a school builds a reliable firewall at the lowest grades, fewer students will reach 4th grade reading at the Below Benchmark level. One 95 Percent Group client in California who has been implementing MTSS districtwide for a few years reported that the district had *no* intervention groups in 4th grade in its fourth year of implementation—an incredible accomplishment!

Best Practices in Administration of Assessments

There are four key decisions schools should make while launching progress-monitoring practices:

1. Determine how often to administer progress-monitoring assessments.
2. Decide which assessment tool is the best to use for each skill group.
3. Determine who will administer the progress-monitoring assessment.
4. Put in place practices to ensure that the data are accessible to all who need it, and encourage optimum use of the data.

In terms of frequency, the most common practice is to assess students in intervention groups every two, three, or four weeks. Every two or three weeks seems optimal. Four weeks is too long a period for moving students up when they have mastered the skill, and it's also too long for recognizing and acting when a student hasn't made enough progress. Weekly assessment is too frequent because it takes away from instructional time when assessing all students in intervention. Regardless of the period chosen, some students *do* need weekly progress monitoring. When a student's data move up and down, it's impossible to get a reliable trend line without more data points. A lack of progress is an early warning sign that the student may later be referred for special education evaluation, so having additional data points can help the team.

It's better to monitor progress less frequently during the first year of MTSS implementation, until teachers are fully engaged in using the data to make decisions on grouping and instruction. It's a good thing when teachers advocate for more frequent progress monitoring because it means they find the data useful. The risk of monitoring too frequently is teacher frustration if they feel too much time is being wasted on assessing. If they are using the data, this complaint rarely comes up.

Finding the right frequency of progress monitoring is like finding the point when a balance board is level. For progress monitoring, it's the point where there is neither too much nor too little. If the school assesses every three weeks, then there are approximately eight progress-monitoring cycles per academic year in addition to the three benchmark periods (BOY, MOY, and EOY). Assessing every three weeks means teachers are monitoring progress four times between the BOY and MOY benchmarks, and four additional times between MOY and EOY. This frequency seems doable because teachers are monitoring only the students who are receiving intervention.

> Finding the right frequency of progress monitoring is like finding the point when a balance board is level.

The second overall decision related to progress monitoring is which assessment tool to use, which was discussed earlier in this chapter. The key is to choose the assessment instrument that most closely measures what the group's been learning.

The third decision is *who* should administer the progress-monitoring assessment. Our recommendation is that the teacher instructing each skill group should assess the students in her group. It's preferable for each teacher to see which students are ready to exit and also to observe what a child is missing if he needs another round in that skill.

The fourth point is to ensure that the data are easily accessible and widely used. Achieving these goals depends upon whether teachers have the knowledge and time to use the data. Learning to use MTSS data takes practice, coaching, and support. Investing in professional development is well worth it, as I discuss in Chapter 9.

There is one last caution to keep in mind about administration of assessments. It's important to monitor progress with an alternate form after the initial assessment. Testing with the same probes used a few weeks earlier may lead to misleading data; some students may simply remember what they saw before. Teachers need to identify any student who isn't moving up in comparison to peers in the group who have been receiving the same high-quality intervention instruction and are moving up. At some point, lack of progress in spite of quality instruction is a warning flag that the student should be tested for a possible learning disability.

Implementation Challenges

Certain challenges come up over and over again when schools are in their first year of MTSS implementation. The first challenge is how to deal with a student who is reading so far below grade level that she is studying completely different skills in her intervention group and during core instruction. During the 30 minutes of daily intervention, the student gets what she needs, but when she returns to core instruction, the material is much too hard. The best option is for the student to be in Tier 3 with more time in the small-group setting, and potentially receiving instruction in an alternate core program.

The second challenge is having enough staff to teach all the deficient skills identified by the diagnostic assessment. On 95 Percent Group's phonological awareness diagnostic assessment, a total of 25 PA skills can be tested. Kindergarten students would never be tested at one time on all 25 skills because some skills wouldn't be taught until the second half of the year. Syllable level is all that's expected until about October, and then onset-rime before the

December break; the 11 phoneme-level skills are not assessed until January. Even then, about 14 skills need to be mastered during the first half of kindergarten. There's no way a school has the resources to teach 14 different PA groups. The solution is to cluster the skills when determining groups; in this example, there could be two levels of syllable groups and one level of onset-rime, for a total of three PA groups.

A third challenge is how to ensure good communication between the intervention teacher and the classroom teacher. It can be very frustrating for a classroom teacher to have no idea how a child is doing during 30 minutes of the day. This challenge is not new. In schools that receive Title I funds, it's always been challenging for the Title I teacher to communicate with the classroom teacher about what occurs during pull-out time. The Walk-to-Intervention model ensures more communication than pull-out models because teachers must collaborate to place students in initial groups and move them after each progress-monitoring cycle. Schools often improve communication by giving everyone access to the data on a spreadsheet located on a school server. One Florida district also created a paper folder for each student where assessment recording sheets are stored, along with notes from the intervention teacher. When a student moves to a new group, the folder is passed to the new intervention teacher. The homeroom teacher can view the folder at any time.

In spite of challenges, regular progress monitoring, with good communication practices, leads to better student results.

Summing Up

Progress monitoring is one of the key processes to include when implementing an MTSS program. Schools should be aware, however, of two common mistakes. The first one is choosing the wrong instrument. The most effective instrument is the one that most closely measures the skill that the instructor is teaching. The second common mistake is failing to adequately use the progress-monitoring data to guide instructional decisions for individual students or failing to view the effectiveness of the entire grade level's tiers of intervention through an "effectiveness report."

Another important consideration related to progress monitoring is the importance of following best practices in assessment administration, including practices related to frequency of assessment, choice of assessment tools, determining who will do the assessing, and ensuring that data are accessible and used effectively. Challenges that schools are likely to face are related to how to accommodate students who are far below benchmark level, providing sufficient staffing for intervention, and ensuring good communication between intervention and classroom teachers.

5

Success Factor #5

Flood the Intervention Block
with Extra Instructors

Schools that are achieving remarkable gains through MTSS are flooding intervention blocks with all the extra help they can gather. What does *flood* mean in this context? It means scheduling every possible person who can teach an intervention group into the 30-minute intervention time slots. Assigning more staff enables more specific skill grouping as well as smaller groups.

Number of Staff Needed

Here is a good rule of thumb for staffing: to implement the recommended Walk-to-Intervention model, schools need *at least* 50 percent more assistants or support staff than the number of classroom teachers. This means that if there are four classroom teachers, at least six instructors will be needed; if there are six classroom teachers, at least nine instructors will be needed, and so on. *Exceeding* the 50 percent rule of thumb for extra instructors will lead to even better results.

The term *instructors* refers to classroom teachers plus any reading specialists, special education teachers, Title I teachers, instructional aides, paraprofessionals, and so on. The phrase "the more the merrier" is appropriate here.

Small group size *does* matter in getting the best results. The further behind grade level the focus skill, the smaller the group should be. Let's look at an example for a school that has four kindergarten homerooms, 84 kindergarten students, and six intervention teachers, including the four

To implement the recommended Walk-to-Intervention model, schools need *at least* 50 percent more assistants or support staff than the number of classroom teachers.

classroom teachers and two other staff members. Imagine that it's February, and the focus skills and group sizes are as follows:

- Benchmark group—30 students
- Sight word group—26 students
- Phonemic manipulation (addition, deletion, and substitution)—16 students
- Phonemic segmentation and blending group—5 students
- Phoneme isolation and categorization group—4 students
- Rhyming group—3 students

The three groups at the top are the students at, or close to, benchmark. The three groups at the bottom are the furthest from benchmark, so they have the fewest number of students, which enables more teacher feedback and practice cycles. For every instructor added, the group sizes improve; if a seventh instructor is available, it would be possible to break up the phonemic-manipulation group of 16 students into two groups of 8.

Possible Intervention Group Instructors

Because each additional instructor enables improvements in group size, let's look at who can help teach a group. After classroom teachers, the first resource to include is Title I teachers if the school is receiving federal funds to hire staff dedicated to supporting students who come from households with incomes below the government-identified poverty level. Before MTSS/RTI became popular, typical school practice was for Title I teachers to pull selected students from their homeroom class and work with them in small groups. The goal was to assist students who enter school with disadvantages compared with their peers whose families have more financial resources. One of the paradigm shifts of MTSS is the opportunity to fully integrate all the services that struggling readers receive. That goal is clear in the California Department of Education's definition of MTSS provided in the Introduction to this book. The first bullet point in the definition is "focusing on aligning the entire system of initiatives, supports, and resources." It speaks about aligning resources, integrating support, and challenging the way school staff have traditionally worked.

Another resource for intervention groups is special education teachers. If they have more time after scheduling all their prescribed Individualized Education Plan (IEP) minutes, they can teach intervention groups. Additionally, federal law permits instruction of non-IEP students in groups with those who have an IEP; these group minutes *do* count toward the IEP required number of minutes.

Speech-language pathologists are uniquely prepared to teach phonological-awareness intervention groups. They also support the MTSS team by reminding teachers who never had linguistic training how to properly pronounce the speech sounds. Teachers who work with English language learners (ELLs) typically teach groups as well. Some schools use the teachers who teach the areas called "specials" in elementary schools. These include music, gym, library/media center, and art teachers. The music teacher can include rhyming, and the gym teacher can have students up and moving while working on speech sounds and oral language; these teachers can also help students master common nonphonetic sight words that need to be memorized, or read aloud and talk through comprehension questions with the benchmark students.

Principals who are recognized as leaders make intervention a whole-school effort. They can be masterful in using school-funding sources to get the maximum resources for lowering group sizes. Some have used their funding to hire double the number of interventionists and have them work half-days rather than all day. For example, if a school has funding for two full-time interventionists, it's possible to plan four intervention blocks in the morning for K–3 and hire four morning-only intervention aides. These aides rotate between grade levels to support the 30-minute blocks during the morning.

Summing Up

The fifth success factor for MTSS implementation is "flooding" a grade level with all possible interventionists. Our recommended rule of thumb is to assign 50 percent more instructors than the number of classroom teachers. Schools are creative in looking to all possible staff members who can teach groups. Additionally, principals getting good results are spending funds in ways that schedule more instructors to be available at the critical intervention blocks, such as funding twice as many half-day morning positions instead of half the number of full-day assistants. This "all hands on deck" approach enables smaller group sizes so that students get more feedback and practice.

6

Success Factor #6

Use Intervention Time Wisely

For struggling readers, intervention time is precious. A dictionary definition of the word *precious* is "of high value not to be wasted or treated carelessly." That pretty much captures the message. Struggling readers are under a deadline—they urgently need to catch up to grade level, and there are only so many resources a school has to devote to any one student. Too many times students are sitting in an intervention group where they already know what is being taught. In Chapter 1, I shared the story of Amy, the student who was rattling off the correct answer to every question. She needed to be in a group that met her needs, and her spot should have gone to a student who needed that particular lesson. In cases like this, having one fewer group member enables the teacher to give more feedback to the other students who *do* need it.

Why Intervention Time Is Precious

Every minute of intervention time is valuable to struggling readers because they're in a race to reach benchmark earlier rather than later. Closing the gap to benchmark as early as possible raises the probability that they will remain at benchmark with Tier 1 core instruction only. Delivering instruction to groups of five or fewer students is costlier than whole-class instruction. Given the high cost and the urgency to get results early in students' elementary years, it's critical to get instruction correct from the outset.

> Struggling readers are under a deadline—they urgently need to catch up to grade level, and there are only so many resources a school has to devote to any one student.

What are the characteristics that make intervention instruction effective? First, the instruction is targeted at exactly the skill the student needs right now. It's like the "just right" chair for Goldilocks. During the rest of the day, a struggling reader isn't experiencing the type of feedback loop that's possible when she's with an instructor who has a laser focus on one skill and is working with only a handful of students. During whole-class instruction, when her 25 classmates are present, her teacher can't stop to correct each mistake she makes. Teachers have to teach to the average, or the middle, of the class during whole-class instruction. During the majority of the school day, the struggling reader receives little or no feedback on her mistakes.

> During the majority of the school day, the struggling reader receives little or no feedback on her mistakes.

For feedback to be worthwhile, it has to be specific and contain information about *why* that answer is not correct. Imagine a struggling reader named Garrison. During whole-class instruction, when he repeatedly gives incorrect answers, the teacher stops calling on him (if he even bothers to raise his hand). The teacher is worried that his incorrect responses might confuse others or embarrass Garrison. She can hear his repeated mistakes, but she can't stop and address them at that very moment. On the other hand, when Garrison is in an intervention group of five students, he gets the kind of feedback that can help him correct his misunderstandings.

Let's consider a type of teacher-student interaction that we'll call a "feedback loop." The teacher asks the small group a question, and Garrison provides an incorrect answer. The teacher responds by giving him an explicit explanation of what is wrong with his answer, and then she models the correct answer with that same word. The next step is critical. Before moving on, his teacher gives him a different word and asks him to try it again. If his answer is incorrect again, she models the right answer with that second word, and he tries it again. The teacher stays with him by explaining it, modeling it, letting him practice, and giving him feedback each time until he gets it. This feedback loop just can't happen during whole-class instruction for every student who makes a mistake. Teachers depend on kids to figure it out by paying attention to the other kids who got the answer right or by listening to a correction of another student, but this requires inferences that struggling readers may not be able to make.

Using Skills Continuums to Place Students in Appropriate Groups

Educators tend to use the words *sequence* and *continuum* interchangeably. In this book, they refer to the same thing—a series of skills arranged in an intentional order from simplest to most complex. Phonological awareness and phonics continuums provide a research-based sequence of the order in which students acquire skills. A continuum shows the order of skill development according to research. Therefore, a continuum displays skills in order from easiest to hardest.

When students are struggling, it's beneficial to use a developmental progression whereby the easiest skills are taught first. Mastering the easier skills first gets the student ready for the difficult ones. Many times, the most difficult skills are multistep processes involving some of the lower skills.

The sequence of phonological awareness skills is well researched. Dozens of research studies have examined the order in which preschoolers become aware of units of sounds in words. Young children develop syllable awareness before onset-rime (rhyming) awareness, which typically develops before phoneme awareness. According to Gail Gillon (2004), an expert on phonological awareness, "Phonological awareness is a multilevel skill, typically seen as comprised of syllable awareness, onset-rime awareness, and phoneme awareness" (p. 11). Citing a number of studies, Gillon says, "Research has confirmed a developmental progression in phonological awareness; an awareness of larger units in words develops prior to awareness of smaller units" (p. 38).

Syllables are larger sound units than onsets and rimes. Phonemes are the smallest units, representing every individual sound in a word. Note that phonemes are the *sounds* in a word, and the number of phonemes is not necessarily the number of letters. Figure 6.1 shows examples of words with a different number of sounds and letters.

A research-based phonological-awareness continuum displays skills in order from syllables to onset-rimes to phonemes. Each of these three main levels has numerous subskills under it.

FIGURE 6.1
Number of Phonemes and Letters in Sample Words

Word	Number of Phonemes	Phonemes	Number of Letters	Letters
mom	3	/m/ /o/ /m/	3	m-o-m
ship	3	/sh/ /i/ /p/	4	s-h-i-p
shape	3	/sh/ /a/ /p/	5	s-h-a-p-e

In its continuum for phonological awareness, 95 Percent Group includes 26 subskills, as shown in Figure 6.2. The continuum shows 11 subskills at the phoneme level. They can be divided into two categories:

- Single phoneme level
  - Phoneme isolation
  - Phoneme identification
  - Phoneme categorization (two skills)
- All phonemes
  - Phoneme blending
  - Phoneme segmentation (two skills)
  - Categorization by number of sounds
  - Manipulation: phoneme addition
  - Manipulation: phoneme deletion
  - Manipulation: phoneme substitution

The three manipulation skills are the highest-level skills, with phoneme substitution as the most complex one and therefore appearing as the last subskill in the continuum. Here's an example of how a teacher might call for phoneme substitution:

- Say the word *bus*.
- Now say it again and change the /s/ to /g/. What's the new word? [bug]

The phoneme manipulation involves the following four lower-level skills:

- Isolating the final sound: /s/
- Deleting it
- Adding a different sound: /g/
- Blending the sounds together

FIGURE 6.2

A Continuum of Subskills for Phonological Awareness

Phonological Awareness

Skill 3 Syllables	Skill 4 Onset-Rime	Skill 5 Phonemes

Compound Words
Segmentation/Blending (3.1)

Application:
Identification (3.2)
Categorization: Position (3.3)

Manipulation:
Addition (3.4)
Deletion (3.5)
Substitution (3.6)

Noncompound Words
Segmentation/Blending (3.7)

Application:
Counting (3.8)
Categorization: Number (3.9)

Onset-Rime
Blending (4.1)
Segmentation (4.2)
Isolation (4.3)

Application:
Identification (4.4)
Categorization (4.5)

Manipulation:
Substitution (4.6)

Single Phoneme
Isolation (5.1)

Application:
Identification (5.2)
Categorization: Position (5.3)
Categorization: Exclusion (5.4)

All Phonemes
Blending (5.5)
Segmentation (5.6 & 5.7)

Application:
Categorization: Number (5.8)

Manipulation:
Addition (5.9)
Deletion (5.10)
Substitution (5.11)

Source: 95 Percent Group's Advanced Phonological Awareness Continuum, Copyright © 95 Percent Group. All rights reserved. Reprinted with permission.

Gail Gillon (2004) explains the difficulty of phoneme substitution this way:

Tasks that require only one operation, such as segmenting, blending, or isolating a sound, are classified as simple phoneme awareness tasks. Tasks that require two operations, with the results from the first operation being held in memory while the second operation is performed (e.g., phoneme manipulation), are classified as compound phoneme awareness tasks. (p. 8)

Using a phonics continuum serves the same purpose as the PA continuum. Both of them sequence the skills from easier to harder.

Once teachers see the PA and phonics continuums, they often comment that their core program doesn't teach the skills in this sequence. Sometimes the same lesson even has a mixture of skill levels. For example, in a kindergarten whole-class lesson, students may be asked to do a rhyming task and a syllable task back to back. Here is an example of two tasks that mix PA levels:

- How many syllables are in the word *handshake*? (two)
- Which two words rhyme? *Cat, mat, mouse* (*cat* and *mat*)

The students who are progressing normally in their development of phonological awareness may have no confusion or difficulty with this mixture of levels in the same lesson. They have enough awareness of the sound structure of language to flip back and forth between levels. However, the students struggling with phonological awareness may find this very confusing. Sequence matters a lot for those who are struggling.

Research on Eliminating Phonological Deficits

Hundreds of research studies have examined which instructional approaches lead to the greatest student gains. These studies answer questions about whether intervention can close student gaps. One expert explains it like this:

> We have ample research to show that by making changes in our instructional approaches, we can prevent many reading difficulties as well as substantially accelerate the reading growth of most students with reading difficulties. (Kilpatrick, 2015, p. 23)

The research supports not only the contention that intervention works, but also that some intervention instruction is more effective than others. Kilpatrick (2015) expresses this point in these two quotes:

> Early, explicit, and systematic instruction in phonics, along with direct instruction in phonological awareness, can prevent reading difficulties and can also remediate reading difficulties. (p. 25)

> The highly successful intervention results involved eliminating the phonological awareness difficulties in . . . weak readers. Other intervention studies that did not eliminate phonological awareness deficits had less impressive outcomes. (p. 66)

No matter what the student's age, grade level, or reason for reading difficulties, failing to eliminate a PA deficit will lessen the impact of small-group instruction. Regardless of what is taught in intervention, if the student has a PA deficit that is not addressed, any instruction provided will be less effective.

Kilpatrick summarized the body of research in a meta-analysis that compiled results across multiple studies; he determined that if the PA instruction never enables students to master phoneme substitution (e.g., *bus* to *bug*), their ability to teach themselves new words will suffer.

Phoneme substitution is one of the most efficient ways to figure out new words; to figure out the unknown word *sake*, for example, one could analyze how it's similar to the known word *lake*. If a reader can't do the phoneme substitution in his head without print, then it's unlikely he'll be able to do it with print.

Mastery Instead of Exposure

Intervention time provides a struggling reader the opportunity to *apply* skills and not just be exposed to them—another reason such time is precious. For struggling readers, instruction during Tier 1 is like riding down a waterslide; there's no getting off the path once the ride starts. Struggling readers need not only the feedback loop described earlier in this chapter, but also an opportunity to apply the skills. Application leads to mastery and retention.

Early in my work with schools, a fortuitous experience helped me realize how important application is to mastering a new skill. This experience occurred at a school in a suburb of Chicago where the principal was a former science teacher who was very data-driven. In October of the second year of our work together, he told me how frustrated he was about something he saw in the student data; he noted that some kindergarten students who met benchmark on Phoneme Segmentation Fluency (PSF) in late May tested below benchmark at the beginning of 1st grade. It was as though they "had it" and then they didn't. This occurrence is sometimes called "summer slippage."

My hypothesis was that these students didn't retain PSF because they never applied it before summer started. The way to apply PSF is to work on the set of skills right above it. Phoneme substitution is one of those manipulation skills above PSF. To complete a phoneme substitution task, the student *must* use four lower-level skills: phoneme isolation, phoneme deletion, phoneme addition, and blending. My hypothesis was that if kindergarten students (including the struggling students) got through all the phoneme manipulation skills before school ended, then they would retain PSF over the summer. Because this principal was a former science teacher, he loved hypotheses and readily agreed to conduct an experiment to test this one.

The next year, the kindergarten team worked diligently to get *all* students to pass the three phoneme manipulation skills (addition, deletion, and substitution) on a PA diagnostic progress-monitoring assessment. In September, when this group of students entered grade 1, their PSF was tested on the universal screener. The new approach worked! The summer slippage was only 2 percent. This result supported the idea that in order to get kindergartners to retain PSF, they need to apply it in higher-level tasks.

This experiment was particularly satisfying because the demographics of these students made them the "perfect storm" for summer slippage. None of them attended summer school, and nearly all of them grew up in homes where the socioeconomic level was below the poverty line. It was unlikely that someone was actively reading aloud to them and playing oral word games while cruising through the grocery store aisles. If the approach used in the experiment can work for this group of students, then it's likely to work for any students.

Summing Up

Intervention time is precious to the struggling reader. One key to using the time wisely is to use skills continuums to guide decisions about how to deliberately close readers' skill gaps. There is nothing haphazard about this approach. The process is to keep stepping a student up one skill at a time until he reaches benchmark for his grade level. Intervention research validates the notion that to get the best results in later reading development, it's critical to ensure that any phonological awareness deficit is eliminated. Using intervention time wisely also requires providing students an opportunity to master skills and not just be exposed to them.

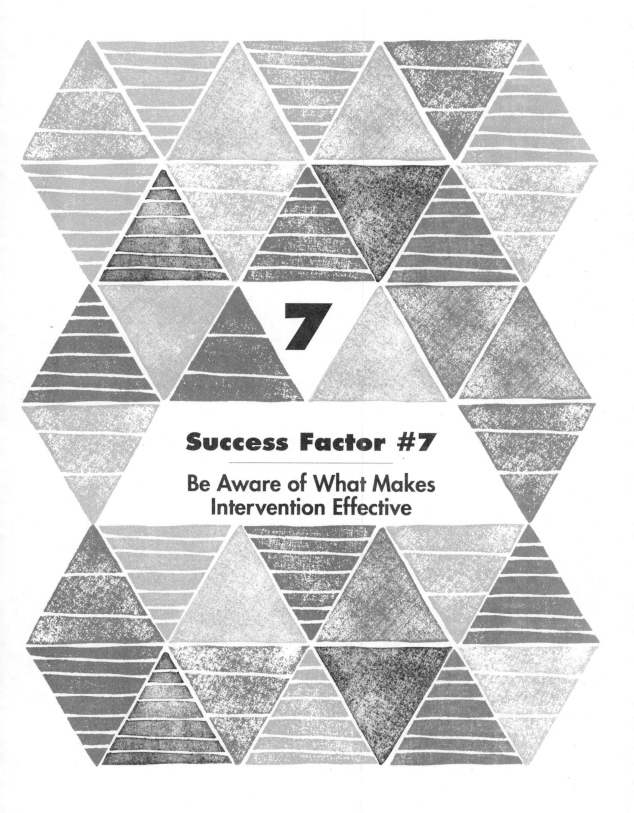

Success Factor #7

Be Aware of What Makes
Intervention Effective

Extensive evidence shows that Tier 2 and Tier 3 intervention instruction delivered in small groups can close the gap for struggling readers. How can effective intervention cause such profound results? What are the characteristics that make it effective? It's not good enough to know that it works; it's critical to understand *why* it works. When teachers don't understand why it works, it's too easy to make adjustments and eliminate something that's essential for strong results. Before you change anything, know what matters.

> It's not good enough to know that intervention works; it's critical to understand *why* it works.

Chapters 1 and 2 included discussion about using diagnostic assessment instruments to pinpoint each struggling reader's lowest missing skill in order to place that student with others who share a common deficit—grouping students in what are referred to as "tight skill groups." Yet it's not as simple as getting the right kids in the right groups. The instruction delivered to each group has to be right also. It's the way the instructor is working with students that leads to profound gains. The focus of this chapter is on what makes intervention instruction effective.

Eight Characteristics of Effective Intervention Instruction

Intervention that is effective has the following characteristics: it is targeted on one skill, teaches skills in a sequence, is explicit, is systematic, incorporates multisensory techniques, uses a feedback loop, involves minimal teacher talk, and follows instructional routines. Let's examine each of these in turn.

1. Targeted on one skill. Intervention time must be focused to be effective. Don't try to simultaneously cover multiple essential components of reading. When too much is covered, a struggling reader doesn't get a chance to master any one thing. Imagine a lesson that spends five minutes on each of the five "pillars" of reading: phonemic awareness, phonics, fluency, vocabulary, and comprehension. It's hard to cover all components in a 90-minute reading block and impossible to do it in a 30-minute intervention block.

If the topic is the phonics *oi/oy* pattern, the entire lesson should be devoted to that skill. The student is explicitly taught that the *oy* spelling is used at the end of a syllable and the *oi* spelling is used when the sound is followed by a consonant. The teacher models with an "I do," which is followed by a "we do"; the final step is the "you do," with the students trying it on their own and receiving feedback. Students have ample opportunity to master understanding this concept by reading and writing pattern words in lists, phrases, and passages. The focus is narrow, but the group won't need to stay on this one pattern for more than a few days, after which students advance to the next missing skill. Focusing on one skill in a lesson gives the student enough time to practice that precise skill until it's mastered. Students should be receiving instruction on the other components of reading instruction, including vocabulary and comprehension, during the core-reading block. The intervention time can be narrowly focused because it's not replacing the core instruction that covers all the other literacy skills.

2. Skills taught in a sequence. Teaching skills in a sequential order is important in intervention instruction. Students are placed in groups based on what they are ready to learn at a particular moment. Diagnostic assessment confirms that the students have mastered the prerequisite skills, or they wouldn't be placed in this group. Rather than assuming that a child knows the easier skills, assessment has confirmed it. Because students know the easier skill, the teacher can drop back down to the easier skill to scaffold a harder skill. For example, when students are having trouble deleting phonemes, the teacher can back up and remind them that it's the same operation that's used with syllable deletion. When the group is struggling in removing the /s/ from the word *stop* to make the word *top*, the teacher can go back to deleting *cow* from *cowboy* to get *boy*. The syllable level is easier than the phoneme level.

With sequential instruction, students are moving along their own personal continuums. They are not asked to do things that are higher than their current level. Think about "perfect practice"; it's not just about practice, it's about *perfect* practice. It stretches the learner a little bit but not too much. Too much is frustrating and too little is boring. It's hard to make gains when instruction is not at the right level. Intervention should have a laser focus on the skill that is located at the place where perfect practice can occur.

3. Explicit instruction. The Reading First federal initiative under No Child Left Behind emphasized the value of explicit teaching. Although participants knew that "explicit" was good, sometimes the attributes that make instruction explicit were lost in the discussion. "Explicit" is the teacher telling the students directly as opposed to assuming they will infer a concept in the lesson. Often educators use the "I do, we do, you do" modeling cycle in teaching lessons. An important hallmark of explicit instruction is the teacher explaining aloud each step during the "I do" portion. A strong "you do" will also include explicit instruction when the student makes a mistake and the teacher provides feedback to each student working on a task in front of her (not independently at their own desks). While giving individualized feedback, the teacher should still use explicit explanations rather than letting the student reach his own conclusions about what he is supposed to do.

4. Systematic instruction. Systematic instruction follows a procedure. Routines provide a consistent procedure because the teacher cues students the same way each time. A benefit of using a routine is that it lowers the cognitive load required by students to figure out what the teacher means when each question is uniquely worded. Asking the question the same way allows students to devote all their attention to solving the task instead of thinking about what was asked. Even if a teacher isn't crazy about routines for many other times of the day, they are helpful during intervention instruction.

5. Multisensory techniques. Multisensory instruction is often associated with instruction for students who are receiving special education services. Manipulatives are helpful in Tier 2 and Tier 3 groups because they make an abstract concept more concrete. A student can use visual cues to see something and not just hear it. Consider this example. When trying to explain why words rhyme, it's much more effective to show students visually that it's the last part of the word that is the same. Imagine a mat with two rows. A picture of a man is placed to the left of the top row, where the word *man* is represented by using two pieces: a small green piece at the beginning to represent /m/ and a larger red piece at the end of the word to represent /an/. When it's time to analyze a second word, a picture of the word *fan* is set below the picture of a man. On the bottom row, a smaller blue piece is placed first to represent /f/, along with a larger red piece for /an/. The two red, larger /an/ pieces are the same size and shape and are displayed one above the other. The teacher points to the smaller green and blue pieces and talks about how the initial sounds in the two words are different. The teacher then points to the two matching, red, larger pieces at the end of each word while explaining that the words rhyme because their ending parts are the same.

> Manipulatives are helpful in Tier 2 and Tier 3 groups because they make an abstract concept more concrete.

Now it's time for students to use manipulatives to represent words. The teacher hands them pictures and asks them to move shapes to build the words *cat* and *bat*. Both the student and the teacher can see whether the larger pieces match for rhyming pairs and don't match for words that don't rhyme.

6. Feedback loops. One of the most significant characteristics in effective intervention instruction is the feedback loop—the cycle that occurs in the small group when a student makes a mistake. There's no delay because the child hears an immediate explanation of what's not right about his answer. Then the teacher models again and explains how the right answer differs from what he said. The teacher gives the student another word, and once again, without delay, he gets immediate feedback on whether he got it right or wrong. If his second attempt is incorrect, the teacher explains and models again. It's called a "feedback loop" because the cycle continues until the student gets it right. But it doesn't stop with one correct answer. The student practices until the new knowledge is assimilated and transferred into long-term memory.

7. Minimal teacher talk. Observing intervention groups reveals a frequent occurrence: teachers doing too much talking. It's important to say something and then stop to let students respond. Don't go on and on before determining whether the students need more explanation. For the most powerful results, teachers should use the minimum number of words and then listen to the students. The more students talk, the more they learn. In a 30-minute lesson, the more times students respond and use manipulatives to solidify their understanding, the more effective the intervention time will be. Repeated practice cycles help students gain confidence and confirm mastery. When teachers ask questions with the minimum number of words, students get more "air time." Routines help remind teachers to minimize the number of words they use to say something.

8. Instructional routines. The benefit of instructional routines is that they reduce the amount of cognitive desk space students have to devote to remembering the instructions. The students' attention can focus not on the instructions but rather on doing the task.

Let's look at an example of a routine. Imagine that a 3rd grade teacher is teaching the consonant-*le* syllable. First, she explicitly defines the syllable type with the following statement: "The pattern for the consonant-*le* syllable type is one consonant letter plus the letter *l* and then the vowel letter *e* at the end. Watch what I do to decide if a syllable is consonant-*le*. This syllable only occurs at the end of a word." The teacher demonstrates, using the following statements:

1. (The teacher holds up a card with the syllable *ble* on it.) Look at this syllable.
2. First I find the vowel letter and touch under it. There is one vowel letter *e*.
3. The *e* follows a consonant plus the letter *l*.
4. The gesture for a consonant-*le* syllable is a box made around the syllable.
5. I place the *ble* card under the column for consonant-*le* syllable.

Now it's time for the students to respond with the teacher while she presents more syllables. Each time, she asks the questions in the same order and with the minimum number of words. Here's the "we do" routine with the student responses in parentheses after the questions:

1. (The teacher holds up a card with the syllable *tle* on it.) Look at this syllable.
2. How many vowel letters? (1)
3. Is it the letter *e*? (yes)
4. Is there a consonant plus the letter *l* before the vowel letter *e*? (yes)
5. Show the gesture for the consonant-*le* syllable. (box around the syllable)
6. Where does the card go? (under the consonant-*le* column)

The routine is repeated at least 20 times with these exact steps, using example and nonexample syllables. This activity should take no more than about five minutes so students get lots of practice in a short time.

Examples of Effective Intervention Instruction

Having described the eight characteristics that make intervention instruction effective, let's look at three examples of what it looks like. The first example is for teaching the phonological awareness skill of rhyming. The second example is about providing phonics instruction with manipulatives to show students how to hear the sounds in a word and then spell it by associating a letter or letter cluster with each sound. The third example relates to teaching students to use the syllable type to figure out an unknown word.

Example 1 — Phonological Awareness

Rhyming can be difficult for some children. If a child still has trouble hearing rhyming words after instruction, keep in mind that this can be a warning sign of a phonological-processing issue. Most students who aren't initially hearing rhymes can learn how to do so with explicit instruction about what part is common in rhyming words. Too often when a student displays a blank expression when asked if the words *ball* and *wall* rhyme, the teacher will say, "Honey, listen. *Baaalll, waaalll.* They rhyme." The teacher says it louder and slower. Yet there is no explicit instruction in that approach. The teacher never tells the student what part of the word *has* to be the same for the words to rhyme. Additionally, the most common instructional materials are activities downloaded from the Internet or taken from an activity book that involve matching pictures of words that rhyme. These activities also don't include explicit instruction.

Activities often involve the following skill levels:

- **Isolation and Segmentation:** Isolate and segment the onset apart from the rime (the rime is the part that rhymes).
  Example: The onset of *ball* is /b/ and the rime is /all/.
- **Rhyme Recognition:** Recognize if two words share a common rime.
  Example: *ball* and *wall*
- **Rhyme Production:** Provide a word that rhymes with a target word.
  Example: *ball* (possible answers: *wall, fall, mall, stall*, etc.)

Figure 7.1 shows an explicit and systematic instructional routine to teach rhyming. It uses manipulatives to make the abstract concept of rhyming concrete for students. Easier skills are taught first. The lesson starts with blending and segmenting the onset away from the rime. Mastering this skill is essential

FIGURE 7.1
Example of Rhyming Instruction

Step	Suggested Teacher Dialogue (with Student Responses in Parentheses)
Introduction	With these manipulatives, I'm going to show you what makes words rhyme. There are two pieces—a smaller green one and a larger red one. When they are pushed together, they represent a whole word.
Blending and Segmentation	In the word *man,* I'm going to separate the /m/ from the /an/. Notice that I pulled the green part to the left while saying /m/ and pointed to the red, larger part while saying the /an/ part.

Rhyme Recognition	• The first word is *man.*
	  – What's the first part? (/m/)
	  – What's the last part? (/an/)
	• The next word is *fan.*
	  – What's the first part? (/f/)
	• Is it the same as /m/? (no)
	  – Do I use green or a different color? (different)
	  – What's the last part? (/an/)
	• Is it the same as /an/? (yes)
	• Do I use red or a different color? (red)
	• *Man* and *fan* rhyme because the last part of the word is the same. See that the last part is red. The pieces look the same. They sound the same: /an/ and /an/ are the same. The words *man* and *fan* rhyme because they have the same last part.
	  – What part's the same in these two words? (the last)
	• Yes, in rhyming the first part is different and the last part is the same.

Rhyme Production	• Would you agree that *man* and *fan* rhyme? (yes) • Now it's your turn. Think of a different word that rhymes with *man* and *fan.* Build it with the colored onset and rime pieces and tell me the word once you're done. (possible answers: *can, ran,* etc.)

Source: From 95 Percent Group Inc., *Phonological Awareness Lessons.* Copyright © 95 Percent Group. All rights reserved. Used with permission.

before moving on to the next higher skill. Although students aren't yet rhyming words, the lesson prepares them for learning to hear and produce rhyming words. According to research, rhyme recognition is easier than rhyme production. Therefore, the skill sequence is to teach recognition before production. The routine uses a minimal amount of teacher talk. When students are asked to respond, they are given two choices rather than a long list of options. The important thing is for the student to focus on determining if the rime is the same or different in two words.

Example 2—Letter-Sound Mapping

One of the most important research-based instructional routines to help students see the correspondence between the sounds in words and the letters that align to the sounds is called "letter-sound mapping." There are several other terms for this instructional approach, such as "phoneme-grapheme mapping" or "orthographic mapping."

The most common way to teach letter-sound mapping is to use something educators call "Elkonin boxes." Elkonin is the name of the individual who developed this instructional strategy. Imagine a mat made on an 8.5-by-11-inch piece of paper positioned in landscape orientation. At the bottom of the page are two rows, each with six equal-sized boxes. Above the rows is a blank area that provides space for laying out colored circular chips to pull down into the boxes while saying the individual sounds in words. Our preference is to consistently place the chips so that consonants start at the top left and vowels are lined up at the top right.

The instructional procedure is to use manipulatives to map the sounds in a word along the top row and then write each letter (or letters) in the box below the sound. Our approach is to use specific colored circular chips or discs. By using specific colors aligned to the sound type, the procedure can be even more valuable because the colors focus the student's attention on the pattern. For example, if blue represents consonants and red represents short vowels, then the word *mom* would be blue-red-blue. The colors point out important phonics patterns; a red vowel followed by one or more blue consonants represents the closed-syllable pattern, and the vowel sound is short.

The instructional routine has several distinct steps. The first step is to place the colored chips that will be needed at the top of the mat and comment on any new color that will be added to teach a new pattern. The teacher says the word and the student repeats it. Then they analyze the word, pull the sound chips into the first row, and write the letters in the second row. Each box represents a sound and not necessarily a letter. Some sounds are spelled with two letters, such as the consonant digraph *ch* in the word *chip* or the vowel team *ee* in the word *green*.

Figure 7.2 shows this instructional routine for four different phonics patterns. There's a reason for every step of the routine, and each step is important.

FIGURE 7.2
Instructional Routine to Teach Phonics Letter-Sound Mapping

Steps	CVC	Consonant Digraph	Long Vowel Silent-e	Vowel Team
SET UP THE MAT: (L = left side; R= right side)				
Place chips.	L: 2 blue consonant chips R: 1 red short-vowel chip	L: 2 blue consonant chips and 1 orange consonant-digraph chip R: 1 red short-vowel chip	L: 2 blue consonant chips R: 1 red short-vowel chip and 1 green long-vowel chip	L: 3 blue consonant chips R: 1 red short-vowel chip and 1 yellow vowel-team chip
Comment on new chip.		New color: Notice I placed a new chip on the left—it's orange.	New color: Notice I placed a new chip on the right—it's green.	New color: Notice I placed a new chip in the vowel area—it's yellow.
SAY THE WORD: "We're going to map the word *xxx.*"				
The word is . . .	*mom*	*ship*	*lake*	*spoil*
Say the word with me.	*mom*	*ship*	*lake*	*spoil*
Finger-stretch it with me. The sounds are . . .	/m/ /ŏ/ /m/	/sh/ /ĭ/ /p/	/l/ /ā/ /k/	/s/ /p/ /oi/ /l/
ANALYZE THE WORD: "Let's determine the number of sounds and boxes."				
How many sounds?	3	3	3	4
How many boxes?	3 (Draw a dark line around the 3 boxes.)	3 (Draw a dark line around the 3 boxes.)	3 (Draw a dark line around the 3 boxes.)	4 (Draw a dark line around the 4 boxes.)
MAP THE SOUNDS: "Let's pull the sounds down."				
Let's pull the sound chips into the boxes.				
First sound?	/m/ (Pull a blue chip into first box.)	/sh/ (Pull down an orange chip.)	/l/ (Pull down a blue chip.)	/s/ (Pull down a blue chip.)
Next sound?	/ŏ/ (Pull a red chip into middle box.)	/ĭ/ (Pull down a red chip.)	/ā/ (Pull down a green chip.)	/p/ (Pull down a blue chip.)
Next/last sound?	/m/ (Pull a blue chip into last box.)	/p/ (Pull down a blue chip.)	/k/ (Pull down a blue chip.)	/oi/ (Pull down a yellow chip.)
Next/last sound?				/l/ (Pull down a blue chip.)
Comments		Notice that I used an orange chip for the first sound. That's because it has an unusual spelling.	Notice that I used a green chip for the middle sound. That's because it's a long-vowel sound.	Notice that I used a yellow chip for the vowel sound. That's because it's a vowel team.

(continued)

FIGURE 7.2 (*continued*)
Instructional Routine to Teach Phonics Letter-Sound Mapping

Steps	CVC	Consonant Digraph	Long Vowel Silent-e	Vowel Team
MAP THE SPELLING: "Now let's spell it."				
Let's write the letters below the boxes.				
How do we spell the . . .	/m/ sound? m	/sh/ sound? sh. I'll write *sh* in the first box.	/l/ sound? l. I'll write *l* in the first box.	/s/ sound? s. I'll write *s* in the first box.
How do we spell the . . .	/ŏ/ sound? o	/i/ sound? i. I'll write *i* in the second box.	/ā/ sound? a. I'll write *a* in the second box and a small *e* in the bottom right corner of the third box.	/p/ sound? p. I'll write *p* in the second box.
How do we spell the . . .	/m/ sound? m	/p/ sound? p. I'll write *p* in the third box.	/k/ sound? k. I'll write *k* in the second box.	/oi/ sound? oi. I'll write *oi* in the next box.
How do we spell the . . .	n/a	n/a	n/a	/l/ sound? l. I'll write *l* in the last box.
What's the word?	*mom*	*ship*	*lake*	*spoil*
How is it spelled?	m-o-m	s-h-i-p	l-a-k-e	s-p-o-i-l
ANALYZE THE WORD: "Let's talk about the spelling of the word *xxx*."				
		Notice that there are two letters in the first box. That's because it takes two letters to spell one sound, the /sh/ sound.	It takes two letters—the letters *a* and *e*. The *a* is in the middle box, and there's a small *e* in the box with the *k*.	Notice that I used a yellow chip for the middle sound. That's because it's a vowel-team sound.
		That's why we use an orange chip instead of a blue one. The orange reminds us that it's an unusual consonant spelled with more than one letter.	We've worked with other sounds that take two letters to spell, but they are in the same box. When we spelled the /sh/ sound, *s* and *h* were in the same box.	
			Why isn't the *e* in a box by itself at the end? If the *e* were in a box by itself, it would spell lakēy.	
			We're going to draw a V-shaped line to connect the letter *a* to the small *e*.	

For example, the process of drawing a box around the number of sounds after counting them limits the number of boxes that can be used when spelling the word. Some sounds are spelled with more than one letter, such as consonant digraphs like *ch* and *sh*, as well as vowel teams like *ee* and *oo*. Drawing an outline around the number of sound boxes before spelling helps students avoid mistakes when they begin to think about how to spell each sound. Although there's a one-to-one correspondence in simple phonics patterns like consonant-vowel-consonant (CVC), it's important to repeatedly reinforce the idea that there's one box for each sound and sometimes there will be more than one letter in a box.

What's great about this instructional strategy is that teachers can observe whether students understand the concept; one indicator is when students hold up their fingers while finger-stretching a word. Finger stretching is an instructional strategy whereby students raise their fingers one at a time while saying each sound. If a student holds up an incorrect number of fingers, this could be a warning sign of a hearing or auditory-processing issue. It's hard to spell words correctly if the student isn't hearing the separate sounds in a word. Teachers have to remember to pronounce the sounds correctly (/b/ instead of /buh/). What step makes this instruction change from phonological to orthographic? It's the step of writing the letters in the second row below the sound boxes.

Example 3—Learning to Read Multisyllable Words

The third instructional routine can be taught in small groups but is also appropriate as a daily five-minute supplement to the Tier 1 core curriculum. This routine was developed to solve a common issue. When schools are initially implementing MTSS at the K–3 level, there can be an overwhelming number of students already in 3rd grade who should have received phonics intervention in 1st and 2nd grade. Teachers of 3rd through 5th graders have a lot of students that they need to fast-track at the same time in order to reduce the number who will need Tier 2, small-group intervention. When 50 percent or more of the students in a classroom are not accurately and fluently reading multisyllable words, enough students need intervention to merit teaching these routines to the whole class for five minutes a day. Although this whole-class instruction will be enough for the majority of the students, there will always be some who still need small-group intervention to attain mastery.

This routine shows students how to use a process to figure out a longer word they don't recognize. Students learn to quickly divide the unknown word into syllables and then use the syllable type to decide whether to use a long or short (or other) vowel sound when they pronounce the word. Even if they don't pronounce the vowel perfectly on the first try, the goal is to increase the probability that the pronunciation will be close enough to recognize the word, assuming that it's in the student's oral vocabulary.

The six syllable types are taught one at a time, from simplest to most difficult. Here is a recommended order of syllable instruction:

1. Closed syllable
2. Long vowel silent-*e* syllable
3. Open syllable
4. Vowel team syllable
5. Consonant-*le* syllable
6. Vowel-*r* syllable

Once a syllable is taught, it continues to be included so practice is cumulative. The closed syllable is taught first because it's not only easy, but also the most common syllable in the English language. The second syllable taught is long vowel silent-*e* because it's easy to learn and fairly common. Even though open syllables are the second most common type in English, they are taught third because open syllable is difficult.

The routine has three steps, each requiring one week to teach. Teaching the routine five minutes daily for five days adds up to a total of 25 minutes of instruction for each step. Because each syllable type takes three weeks to teach, instruction on all six can be completed in as little as 18 weeks of school. Teachers follow with a post-test and provide small-group instruction for those who didn't get it with the fast-track, whole-class instruction. Here are the three steps:

1. Recognize the syllable type.
2. Read the syllable.
3. Read a multisyllable word.

In Step 1, students are taught to fluently recognize the syllable without pronouncing it. Single-syllable nonsense syllables are used to avoid presenting words that students already know. Using nonsense syllables levels the playing field so struggling readers and English language learners are not disadvantaged. For example, after the teacher provides an explicit definition of the syllable type and models what to do, she holds up a word card with the nonsense word *sim* on it. She asks if this is, or is not, a closed syllable. Students say the syllable type aloud and show a hand gesture so teachers can see that all students are engaged and answering correctly.

Step 1 develops mastery of syllable-type recognition, and in Step 2 students learn to pronounce the vowel correctly based on syllable type. One-syllable nonsense words are used again in the second step, but this time students are cued to say the vowel sound and then read the syllable.

In Step 3, students learn the proper place to divide a nonsense two-syllable word. The second syllable is covered while students are prompted to read the first syllable, and then the same process is followed with the second syllable. For each syllable, students are prompted with three cues: name the syllable type, say the vowel sound, and then read the syllable. After reading each syllable separately, the two parts are put together to read the entire word. Once students have mastered the process with two-syllable nonsense words, multisyllable real words are read. Figure 7.3 shows the routine for Step 3.

FIGURE 7.3
Instructional Routine for Reading Multisyllable Words, Step 3

Components of Step 3	Teacher Dialogue	Student Response
Example: *simdap*		
Determine the number of syllables.	• Pretend to touch the vowel letters. – How many vowel sounds? – How many syllables?	Point to *i* and *a* 2 2
Divide the word.	• How many consonants between the vowel sounds? – Where do we divide the word?	2 Between the *m* and the *d*
Read the first syllable.	• First syllable – Syllable type? – Sound? – Read the syllable.	Closed (closed-fist gesture) /ĭ/ *sim*
Read the second syllable.	• Second syllable – Syllable type? – Sound? – Read the syllable.	Closed (closed-fist gesture) /ă/ *dap*
Put the word together.	• Read the whole word. • Read it again, faster.	*simdap* *simdap*

Source: From 95 Percent Group Inc., *Multisyllable Routine Cards.* Copyright © 2010–2017 by 95 Percent Group Inc. All rights reserved. Used with permission.

The reason this particular instructional routine works when taught as a whole-class supplement is because it's quick and engaging. Some teachers ask whether it's a waste of time for the students who already successfully read multisyllable words. Some students intuitively figure out a lot of the patterns, but often they don't know why they read a syllable that way. This instructional routine explains why words are read the way they are. Because it's taught for only five minutes a day, it's not taking much time away from other instruction. It's engaging because it's fast paced, it uses gestures, and working with nonsense words makes it feel almost game-like. The teacher talk is minimal, so students are doing the majority of the talking, with many chances to respond each minute. Kids like it. Teachers report that if they forget to do the routine one day, the students will remind them. Training science and social studies teachers on the routines is advantageous so that consistent cues can be used on the longer complex words in these other content areas.

A Caution About Using Intervention Techniques with the Whole Class

A serious concern emerges when schools try to use intervention instruction for whole-class instruction but omit some key attributes of what makes the instruction effective. The intention is good, but the outcome is bad. This shift to the whole class happens because after exposure to effective intervention strategies, teachers realize that their Tier 1 core program lacks the kind of explicit instruction that they are teaching in the Tier 2 and Tier 3 small groups. They see that students in intervention groups are mastering these skills, so they believe that if they use these instructional strategies with their whole class, all students will benefit.

One day while I was visiting an Arizona client school, the reading coach was excited to show me that they had figured out a way to teach 95 Percent Group's *Phonics Chip Kit* to the whole class. This material, which was described in Example 2 earlier in this chapter, was designed for small intervention groups and never intended for whole-class instruction. The reading coach had arranged the schedule so that we would spend about 15 minutes in two 2nd grade classrooms, both teaching the same lesson, which was the *oi/oy* vowel team. The first classroom had students gathered on the floor at the front of the classroom, and the teacher was teaching the lesson on the interactive whiteboard so they could all see it. After she modeled the lesson, she called one student at a time up to the interactive whiteboard to move the chips by sliding a finger across the screen. This was ineffective for two reasons; there's no evidence that moving a chip on a whiteboard is the same as the kinesthetic process of sliding physical chips, and nearly all the other students were not paying attention when the one student was at the whiteboard.

In the second classroom, the teacher taught with "I do" and "we do" by moving pieces on an overhead projector. Following the teacher's demonstration, the 24 students were supposed to complete the "you do" in 12 pairs at desks. Because so many colored phonics chips are needed for the instructional routine, it's sold as a kit with a storage case and eight copies of laminated student chips for a small group and not a full classroom. The *oi/oy* lesson requires a mat and eight colored chips for each student. Because of the quantity of chips to manage, the teacher had eliminated one chip, which was the blank yellow chip. The instructional technique involves pulling a blank yellow chip down first; then depending upon whether or not there's a consonant after the yellow chip, either the *oi* or the *oy* spelling chip substitutes for the blank yellow chip. The word *boy* is spelled with the letters *oy* at the end of the syllable, whereas the word *boil* uses the *oi* spelling because there's a consonant letter *l* after the /oi/ sound. The teacher had eliminated the most critical chip. By forcing the students to choose the *oi* or *oy* spelling before seeing if there is a consonant after that sound, the entire lesson was ruined. Additionally, because students were working in pairs, each child had less opportunity to practice with hands on the chips.

This is an example of how moving instruction to a whole-class setting left behind one of the very attributes that makes this instruction so effective in small groups. It's impossible to use the manipulatives in the same way when the lesson is taught to 20 or more students versus 5 students in a small intervention group. Research on the efficacy of the instruction has shown the importance of students moving manipulatives. Therefore, eliminating that part when it's taught to the whole class removes a critical piece, and there's no way to know if the instruction will be effective when this change is made.

In addition to the manipulatives, one of the things that makes Tier 2 and Tier 3 instruction effective is the feedback loop. Because instruction takes place in a small group, the teacher can respond to an error by immediately explaining what's wrong and modeling the correct version again. Then the student practices it again right away, with the teacher watching to make sure he got it right. That individualized feedback loop just can't occur when the instruction is directed to the whole class.

One more caution is important to note. Be careful to realize the difference between instructional *strategies* and *activities*. A lot of activities, games, worksheets, and graphic organizers can be downloaded for free from the Internet or found in books. Activities are useful for practicing after explicit instruction, but too often teachers don't recognize that activities alone do not ensure results like those that can be expected from explicit instruction.

Summing Up

Effective intervention instruction has eight characteristics: it is targeted, sequential, explicit, systematic, and multisensory; and it uses feedback loops, minimal teacher talk, and instructional routines. The instructional routine for reading multisyllable words can be used in a whole-class setting, as well as the typical small-group setting used for intervention. But caution is advised for using intervention techniques for whole-class instruction, because often the very characteristics that make the techniques effective can't be used with a large number of students.

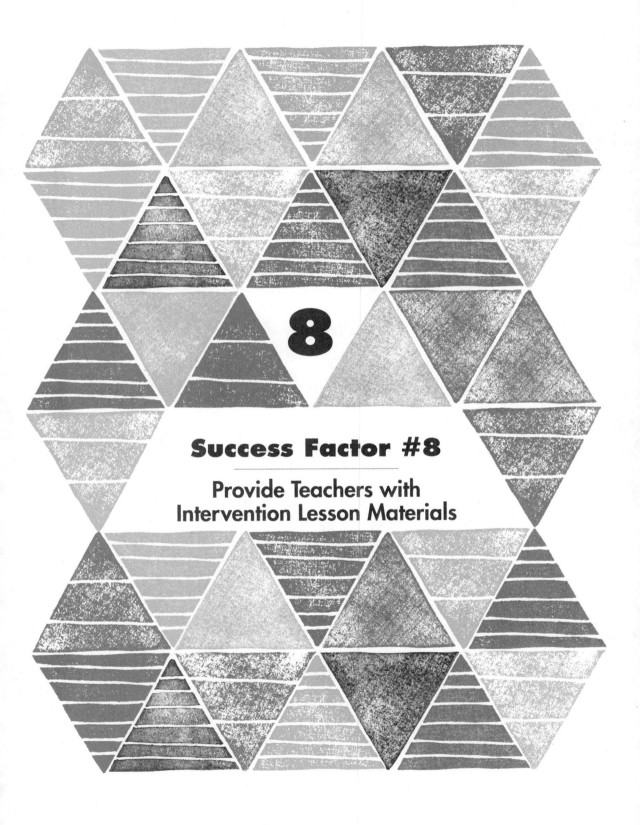

8

Success Factor #8

Provide Teachers with
Intervention Lesson Materials

The Seattle Public Schools has a blog called the *Seattle Schools Community Forum*, where a January 2016 post was titled "MTSS—The Unfulfilled Promise." A teacher named Charlie Mas expressed a frustration that many teachers in districts throughout the United States are feeling. It's not that they don't believe in MTSS or don't want to do it; they simply don't have the time to create all the lessons that are needed. Here are Charlie's words, excerpted from his original post and his responses to reader comments:

> The MTSS process may sound simple or even just sound like good teaching practice, but it is not only really hard, it is a huge amount of work. While the district and the school have a part to play, the bulk of the work falls on the teacher. . . .
>
> MTSS has worked, but only when the commitment was made by the teachers in the school. We have examples of this in Seattle. Mercer [School] was such a school at one time. They were able to do it thanks to charismatic leadership and a cadre of teachers who all committed to the strategy. This is not a scalable process, yet the District talks about taking it to scale. . . .
>
> For it to work the district (or someone) would have to create all these little, tailored lessons like additional skill practice in a specific skill like long division . . . I think this may be one of the really big problems with the MTSS implementation: this district hasn't built the catalog of lessons. Instead, they are relying on the teachers to create them. (Mas, 2016)

For districts to take MTSS to scale, it is critical to provide teachers with many things, including data, intervention time built into the schedule, professional development, collaboration time, and materials. Providing teachers with lessons is one of the 10 critical factors that are the focus of this book. Yet not all lessons are created equal. Some are more effective than others, and in this chapter we will explore why that is so.

Characteristics of Effective Intervention Lessons

Many lessons are available on the Internet, where some sites feature teacher-created lessons that can be purchased for a small fee and others offer lessons that can be downloaded and used for free (*Engage NY* is an example of a free site; see https://www.engageny.org). Although these sites have some excellent lessons, using these lessons for intervention may not result in large student gains like those described in this book.

Successful intervention lessons have the following characteristics:

• Lessons are organized in a carefully designed sequence, with lessons available to cover each skill.

• Lessons are tied to diagnostic assessment (for example, in 95 Percent Group's PSI, Skill 5.2 is *long*-i *silent*-e on both the phonics diagnostic screener and the phonics intervention lessons).

• Manipulatives are available to support instruction for all students in a small group.

• Research-based strategies are at the heart of the lesson.

• Routines are used throughout lessons to minimize time spent on teaching new practices for each lesson.

The following sections include a description of each characteristic, along with an explanation of its importance.

A Carefully Designed Sequence

Sequential is one of those attributes like *explicit*: it's highly acclaimed and poorly understood. The three instructional descriptors emphasized during professional development for Reading First were *explicit*, *sequential*, and *systematic*. For successful intervention, the sequence has to be determined before writing the first word of the first lesson. In this book, sequence is represented in a continuum, which is a visual way of displaying the order of skills, with the easiest on the left and the most complex on the right.

Sequential is one of those attributes like *explicit*: it's highly acclaimed and poorly understood.

Sequence is important for a couple of reasons. First, the more complex skills often include the easier ones. For a 1st grade student to be able to delete phonemes, the precursor skills are to isolate and blend sounds in words. When a teacher asks for the new word that results after /s/ is deleted from the word *stop*, the student has to take the /s/ sound off the beginning and blend the remaining sounds to get the new word, *top*.

Another reason sequence is important in the design of intervention lessons is the cumulative use of the words in passages that enable practice on the focus skill and previously taught skills. In a typical phonics sequence, short vowels are taught before long vowels. The skills that precede long vowels are short vowels in a consonant-vowel-consonant pattern and short vowels with consonant blends and consonant digraphs. By the time a child reaches a lesson teaching *long vowel silent*-a, he can already read the following types of short-vowel words: *mat*, *sit*, *rub*, *hand*, *jump*, *ship*, and *chick*.

A well-defined sequence is essential for the approach advocated in this book because an intervention group has to be able to start instruction on any skill that's been pinpointed by diagnostic assessment. If assessment confirms that a student knows all the short-vowel patterns but fails to pass the first long-vowel pattern, then the student's instruction begins on *long vowel silent*-e. To achieve the best results, it's critical to skip what the student already knows (in this case, the short-vowel lessons) and start with the lesson that focuses on the student's lowest deficit skill.

The lesson includes many strategies, including sorting words into columns based on whether they have a short or long vowel and reading passages containing words with the focus pattern and all the patterns below the focus skill. Passages that are considered decodable don't include any word pattern that is higher on the continuum (except previously taught nonphonetic sight words) and therefore hasn't been taught yet. Practice in reading word patterns the student already knows is critical for review and retention.

Schools should avoid intervention materials that are designed to require instruction on, for example, the entire 99-lesson program even if the student has mastered some of the lower skills. Likewise, many intervention programs have a placement test and allow only a few entry points. The best approach is to use a phonics program that enables entry at any point in a sequence of 75 to 100 lessons.

Materials that are developed with an approach called "spiraling" also won't work well for intervention. A spiral design includes initial instruction in a lesson, then a gap during which unrelated concepts are covered, and finally the reemergence of the skill many lessons later, with instruction going deeper each time it appears. Because the instruction is broken into many different lessons, the design doesn't work with the intervention approach advocated in this book, which calls for a skill to be taught in one place and practiced until the student reaches mastery. Spiraled instruction is a design for core programs, not intervention.

Alignment with Diagnostic Assessment

One of the most effective designs for MTSS features strong alignment of the diagnostic assessment with the lesson sequence. Teachers appreciate a structure that has transparent alignment from assessment to grouping to instruction.

Let's see how this works using a student example. Vanessa is a new student in Chavez Elementary School in Arizona. Her family has recently moved to a new apartment, and she has just been enrolled in 3rd grade. During the second week of school, her teacher, Miss Hanson, completed assessment with the universal screener that Chavez School uses. She learned that Vanessa's composite score places her in the Well Below Benchmark category. Because her accuracy rate on the Oral Reading Fluency portion was 78 percent compared to the benchmark of 99 percent, Miss Hanson assessed her on the *Phonics Screener for Intervention* (*PSI*), the phonics diagnostic assessment that Chavez School uses.

By testing Vanessa with the *PSI*, Miss Hanson learned that she was at mastery on *short vowels in CVC words* (Skill 2) and *short vowels with consonant blends* (Skill 3). She didn't pass Skill 4, which is *short vowels with consonant digraphs*. Miss Hanson assessed one more skill up the continuum and confirmed that Vanessa didn't pass Skill 5 either, which is *long vowel silent*-e. Therefore, Vanessa will be placed initially in a Skill 4 group with several other 3rd graders who need to master that same skill. One of the other 3rd grade teachers will be teaching Vanessa's group during the 30-minute intervention block, and she'll be starting with the Skill 4.1 lesson from the *Phonics Lesson Library*. After three weeks, the intervention teacher monitors the progress of the students in the group with an alternate Form B of Skill 4 on the *PSI*. They have covered the lessons for Skills 4.1, 4.2, and 4.3. All five students in Vanessa's group are doing well on the end-of-lesson assessment for those three lessons, so they are making progress but are not yet done with consonant digraphs. There are many more consonant digraph skills to be learned, so for the next three weeks, the group will continue up the progression of Skill 4 lessons, and then maybe they can move up to Skill 5.

What teachers like about the scenario just described is that there is no guesswork. The diagnostic assessment pinpoints the lowest missing skill, which becomes the student's starting place. The student is placed with others who have the same need and have passed the lower skills as well. The teacher has clarity about which lesson to use. The numbering system provides a seamless process from assessing to grouping to selecting materials for instruction. Without this seamless process, there's a risk that it will be hard to identify a lesson that matches the need—and then all that work to diagnose and form groups is for naught.

Inclusion of Manipulatives

Research has shown that multisensory reading instruction is the most effective kind for students who are dyslexic. Struggling readers who are not diagnosed with dyslexia also benefit from instruction that gives them the experience of moving manipulatives and making gestures. Students are more engaged and are more likely to retain what they learn if they are *doing* rather than simply listening or watching.

> Students are more engaged and are more likely to retain what they learn if they are *doing* rather than simply listening or watching.

Chapter 7 includes an example of using shapes to teach rhyming. Phonological awareness emphasizes listening and speaking units of words, and the instruction does not include letters. When letters are included, the instruction becomes phonics instruction. Once a student develops a sufficient level of phonological awareness, instruction with letters helps further reinforce phonemic awareness, as students map the letters used to spell sounds.

A variety of objects can help make the abstract phonological awareness concepts more concrete. Sounds in words are very elusive and can be hard for some students to learn. When teachers use pictures and shapes, students can better understand the concept that sounds in a word can be separated into units. Working on a mat or a graphic organizer helps show where manipulatives are placed. When students move manipulatives to specific spots to indicate the location of the sound in the word, both the student and the teacher can see whether the student has reached mastery. Patterns are more obvious when specific colors are used to represent pieces of words. All of these reasons provide a convincing rationale for using manipulatives, but perhaps the best reason is that students stay more engaged when they are doing something physical.

Research-Based Instructional Strategies

Based on our work with educators, perhaps one of the most frequently misunderstood topics is the distinction between evidence and research. During the Reading First implementation, the law emphasized that instruction needs to be "research-based." Later, another term emerged: "evidence-based." Here are the differences:

- **Research-Based**—The instructional strategies included in the instruction have been shown through research studies to result in greater gains for students. The research is typically conducted by objective scientists who study the strategy and publish results about the effectiveness of an instructional approach, such as explicit phonics versus incidental phonics. Usually the research is not related to a specific program but is focused on the strategy.
- **Evidence-Based**—A program has been evaluated within a school setting, and the evidence shows that students did better with this program. Schools compare their population with the students in the study to surmise whether the program will work equally well with their students.

For more information on current definitions, see a publication by the U.S. Department of Education titled "Using Evidence to Strengthen Education Investments" at the following link: https://www2.ed.gov/policy/elsec/leg/essa/guidanceuseseinvestment.pdf.

Use of Routines

An instructional routine is a series of deliberate exchanges that an instructor engages in with students. Each time the routine is taught, it uses the same set of steps delivered in approximately the same way. Routines are comparable to standardized directions on an assessment, although perhaps not quite as rigid. Observing two different instructors teaching the same lesson using a routine, an observer would see the same steps in the same order, using essentially the same language.

The second example in Chapter 7 describes a routine for phoneme-grapheme mapping that can be used for many different phonics patterns. It is important to complete the steps in the prescribed order. Here are the steps:

- Determine the number of sound boxes.
  - Say the word.
  - Finger-stretch it with me.
  - How many sounds?
  - How many boxes?
- Map the sounds.
  - What's the first sound? (Pull sound chip down to first box.)
  - What's the next sound? (Pull sound chip down to second box.)
  - What's the last sound? (Pull sound chip down to last box.)
- Map the letters.
  - How do you spell the first sound? (Write the letter in the box below the first sound box.)
  - How do you spell the second sound? (Write the letter in the box below the second sound box.)
  - How do you spell the last sound? (Write the letter in the box below the last sound box.)
- Say the word.

Routines are important because they

- Minimize the time the teacher spends explaining what to do as the steps become familiar to students and they need less explanation over time.
- Minimize teacher talk and maximize time devoted to student responses.
- Provide structure, so teachers don't forget to complete all the steps.
- Help students know what's coming next, which builds their confidence.
- Free up students' cognitive "desk space" for new learning.

Teachers see the benefit of routines as soon as they notice that students are getting through more examples in each lesson and efficiently mastering the content. There's nothing like progress to encourage teachers that the approach is working!

Summing Up

Teachers have expressed frustration with the demands of creating the types of materials needed to implement MTSS. Schools do need to consider how they will provide lessons. Effective intervention lessons are sequential, are aligned with diagnostic assessment, include manipulatives, are based on research-based instructional strategies, and use routines.

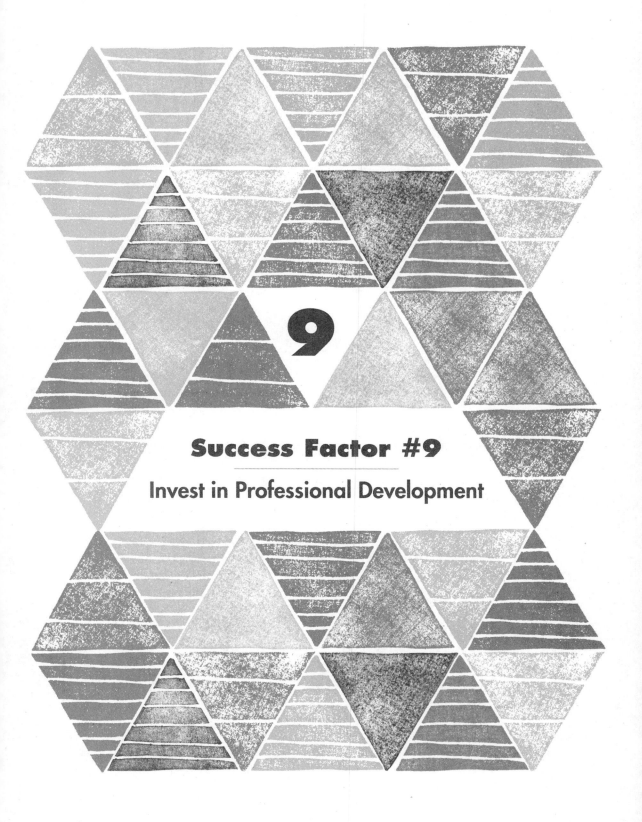

Success Factor #9

Invest in Professional Development

To experience profound gains in student scores from MTSS, professional development is critical. Too many times schools take on an initiative and buy products for teachers without acknowledging that results depend upon teachers implementing new products with fidelity. MTSS in literacy is not about the stuff you buy; it's about implementing new structures, processes, and instructional materials so that the school undergoes a paradigm shift in how teachers identify and address struggling readers.

As discussed in Chapter 8, teachers do need good instructional materials so they have the lessons and manipulatives ready to use in their intervention groups. An essential implementation principle is to provide instructional materials that not only use research-based instructional strategies but also have been shown to be effective, through evidence studies, with students like those in teachers' current classrooms. Yet it's possible to invest in materials that meet the research and evidence requirements and still not see student gains a year or two after implementation.

MTSS requires a comprehensive professional development approach that ensures all staff will implement the needed components. It's not only about the instructional materials, although they are important. And it's not just about administering and using assessment data, although data are also important. MTSS affects the way teachers spend their time, determine what each student needs, and decide what and how they teach

MTSS requires a systemwide change, which means that planning professional development is just as important as selecting assessments and instructional materials.

during key learning time. Getting it right requires an intentional systemic design. The only way to get all staff on board with implementation is to gather them in groups to communicate and engage in dialogue. It's not possible to get really good results if MTSS is only implemented by some teachers in some grade levels. MTSS requires a systemwide change, which means that planning professional development is just as important as selecting assessments and instructional materials.

Professional Development by Role

Consider which school staff members will be affected by MTSS in literacy. When a school implements MTSS, the list of those whose job is affected is long. It includes administrators, reading coaches or specialists, classroom teachers, Title I staff, paraprofessionals who serve as interventionists, special education teachers, and teachers of English language learners. MTSS is one of the most comprehensive initiatives principals will ever implement. It affects the schedule, the way students are grouped, how teachers work together within a grade level, and the instruction students receive. Yet not everyone affected by MTSS needs to know and do the same things. Principals need to have a big-picture sense of what good implementation looks like so they can lead the effort. Reading coaches or specialists, who are the reading experts in the building, need information at a deeper level, and they need it ahead of the teachers so they can support others in their building. Teachers need to learn how to use data to make instructional decisions and how to teach small groups of students who are struggling to succeed.

When it comes to professional development, one size does *not* fit all. Delivering professional development in strands by role is recommended in order to meet the needs of each specific group. Dividing the staff into three groups—administrators, reading coaches, and teachers—is ideal. In large districts, it may be advisable to create a fourth group composed of instructional assistants—the classroom aides who work alongside teachers and often provide small-group instruction. The following sections describe the needs of each group, the recommended content, and the most effective format for professional development.

Professional Development for Administrators

Administrators need to be prepared for their role as the MTSS leader of their building. The most effective approach is to provide them with professional development focused specifically on administrator needs. Too often the education field assumes that principals can simply attend training with their teachers. Administrators do need to know what the teachers are hearing, but they need something different to be a good leader of this initiative. Administrator sessions typically include principals, assistant principals, district literacy leaders, and district or school leaders of special education, Title I, and ELL.

Tailored to their role as the leaders of MTSS, professional development for administrators generally includes the following topics:

- Understanding MTSS goals and objectives
- Knowing state and district MTSS recommendations or requirements
- Building buy-in with staff
- Determining and communicating the rationale for the initiative
- Understanding the building-level decisions for implementation
- Adding intervention blocks to the school's master schedule
- Determining optimal delivery models for Tier 2 and Tier 3 instruction time
- Planning professional development for staff
- Inspecting quality and fidelity of tiers of instruction
- Setting expectations about grade-level analysis and reporting of data on progress

The role of the principal is much different from that of the teachers. That's why it's essential that principals have time together to talk about challenges and successes in fully implementing MTSS in their buildings. Typically, a kick-off meeting for administrators should precede any other professional development. Principals don't want to be in the dark, not knowing what the district is providing their staffs. After the initiative is launched and training of teachers and reading coaches is in process, best results occur when the principals meet periodically. Three times a year for half-day sessions seems to work well. After MTSS is launched, the topics shift to what reports principals should be looking at, how to motivate staff to continue the implementation, and how to observe intervention blocks and look for strengths and opportunities for improvement.

Because initiatives rarely receive immediate buy-in from every teacher, one thing that principals value is talking with their colleagues about how to handle reluctant or resistant teachers. MTSS is not a "one and done" type of initiative. Leaders must identify where to focus efforts in order to deepen the implementation. They also need to continually provide feedback to teachers on the data analysis, the grouping, and the quality of instruction. Adjustments are constant during the first three years, until schools achieve full implementation. Then the focus shifts to sustainability.

During the second and third year of implementation, principals share at a deeper level at the administrator meetings. They need a facilitator who can establish a safe, supportive environment where they can openly discuss challenges. The issues that come up often are how to deal with teachers who continue to be reluctant or resistant, how to get the entire staff to welcome the reading coach entering their rooms and providing mentoring, and how to resolve those challenging scheduling issues.

Through such discussions, administrators can develop trusting relationships with their peers. In a recent article in *American Educator* titled "The Trust Gap: Understanding the Effects of Leadership Churn in School Districts" (Finnigan & Daly, 2017), the authors address the topic of frequent turnover of principals and district leaders and how it leads to the breakdown of trusting relationships. The first paragraph describes the importance of networks of relationships in school buildings:

> As every educator knows, it's important who your colleagues are—fellow teachers and principals alike. . . . It is through these networks that learning takes place, as educators interact with one another, exchanging knowledge, advice, and professional support and engaging in friendships. (p. 24)

The article points out that in trusting relationships, learning happens when teachers and principals allow themselves to become vulnerable by openly sharing their challenges with their colleagues. But with administrative turnover, priorities in districts and schools often change. A common phrase in education is "this too shall pass," and it's used by some teachers to justify closing their doors and doing whatever they want instead of what leaders are asking them to implement.

The study described in the article included qualitative research examining the relationships among leaders—specifically, who they turned to as a source for work-related knowledge and who they turned to for emotional or social support—and how relationships affected reform efforts. The authors found that leaders need colleagues they can reach out to not only for work-related support, but also for emotional support, which is equally important for reform. The authors summarized their insights as follows:

At the heart of forming trusting relationships is the ability to be vulnerable and share, to show respect for others' ideas, and to learn from the knowledge that others bring to an organization. Both innovation and improvement require risk taking and idea sharing, but underlying emotional connections are critical in helping the technical aspects of work to take hold. (Finnigan & Daly, 2017, p. 29)

Professional development for principals and other administrators should nurture an open environment where sharing and mutual respect can lead to stronger networks among them. Leading a school to full implementation of MTSS is not easy. Principals need support from their colleagues at other buildings as well as at the district office.

Professional Development for Reading Coaches

Budgetary constraints have led to a reduction in the number of reading coaches in U.S. schools. From about 2000 to 2008, during the roll-out of the Reading First initiative under No Child Left Behind, there was strong support and funding for reading coaches who mentored colleagues to improve instruction. With tighter budgets, fewer schools now fund this position, which is unfortunate. Achieving and sustaining improvements in literacy within elementary schools without reading coaches is difficult for many reasons, including gaps in classroom teachers' literacy knowledge during preservice training and the effects of constant teacher turnover.

In addition to the challenges of funding reading coaches, role titles can be confusing. Some common titles are reading coaches, instructional coaches, reading specialists, and MTSS or RTI coordinators. A couple of variables affect the role of an individual who holds one of these titles. First, does this individual coach others or only provide small-group instruction to struggling readers? Second, does the person serves as the key literacy advisor to the principal? Most often, if the word "coach" is in the title, the person is mentoring colleagues. When the title is "instructional coach," the educator is likely to be responsible for both literacy and math. When the title is "reading specialist," this person is probably not coaching peers but dedicating most of the day to instructing small groups of students. The title "MTSS or RTI coordinator" may or may not include coaching peers; often this person focuses much more on the student data and getting materials ready for teachers.

When implementing MTSS, principals need to designate one literacy expert to take part in special training over and above what the teachers receive. This professional development is typically funded and directed by the district ELA curriculum department. Outside consultants are often contracted to provide this training and to answer complex literacy questions.

What do the designated building reading experts need in terms of professional development? They need to know more than the teachers, and they benefit from receiving the information ahead of the teachers so that they are in a position to answer questions. It's wise to provide these site-based literacy experts with three full days of training per academic year in addition to having them attend the teachers' training. Here are some typical topics and components to include in reading coaches' professional development:

- More extensive training on how to administer and score all literacy MTSS assessments
- Interpretation of the assessment data used to pinpoint each student's deficit
- Analysis of data to place students in Tier 2 and Tier 3 skill groups
- Evaluation of the effectiveness of Tier 1 in identifying improvements
- Practices for regrouping or periodically moving students between groups
- Extensive training on instructional programs and materials so they can model lessons for teachers
- Discussion around content and facilitation strategies for leading MTSS discussions at grade-level team meetings
- Access to outside experts who can answer complex questions about instruction and assessment

One of the most critical things administrators can do is to set clear expectations for the role of the reading coach or expert. Coaches are peers, not administrators. The teachers need to see coaches as resources and be willing to ask them for feedback and consultation—not just for responses to procedural questions. When principals fail to clarify the coach's role, sometimes coaches overstep the boundary of being a peer and not a supervisor, which can result in damage to relationships.

Professional Development for Teachers

The teacher strand of professional development is different from the strands for reading coaches and administrators. Teachers need to know how to administer and score the assessments, interpret the data, place students in groups, and deliver effective intervention instruction to the Tier 2 and Tier 3 small groups. This strand includes not only classroom teachers but also other instructors whose positions are supported by different monetary sources, such as funding for special education, ELL, and Title I.

One of the great things about the MTSS framework is that it can help a school move away from sending students out of the classroom so that others can address their reading difficulties. This mindset just doesn't produce good results. It leads to students receiving disjointed instruction. Regardless of whether a student is on an Individualized Education Plan (IEP) to receive special education services or is eligible to receive either ELL or Title I services, results are best when the classroom teacher views those other services as integrated into the tiered model and not separate from it. In optimal situations, the classroom teachers are teaching small intervention groups along with other instructors whose positions may be paid by ELL, Title I, or special education funding. These other instructors are under specific federal guidelines that must be followed. However, with good planning, they can work with designated students and have some nondesignated students in their small groups as well. All teachers involved in literacy—whether classroom teachers or teachers funded under special programs—need professional development in MTSS practices and procedures. Professional development for teachers typically includes the following topics:

- Understanding the goals and purposes of implementing an MTSS framework
- Administering and scoring all MTSS assessments
- Using assessment data to pinpoint deficits
- Placing students in Tier 2 and Tier 3 groups
- Evaluating Tier 1 for areas that need to be supplemented
- Participating in meetings about students who are not making progress
- Teaching instructional materials with fidelity

The best approach is to plan for two different formats for teacher professional development: workshop format and coaching format. Topics that can be efficiently covered in a workshop include administering assessments, scoring assessments, and interpreting assessment data, as well as foundational knowledge about the MTSS framework and developing a common language across all teachers. Other topics, including how to improve intervention instruction, are best covered in smaller coaching sessions. These formats and others are covered in greater detail later in this chapter.

Professional Development for Instructional Assistants

Instructional assistants can be critical to getting good results with MTSS. These are the often part-time instructors who are not classroom teachers. In past years, it was common to have assistants in the classroom to help the teacher with things like making copies, walking students to other parts of the building, laying out and putting away materials, and generally doing anything the teacher requested. Now it's rare to see an instructional assistant performing those administrative tasks for the teacher, except maybe in kindergarten classrooms. In today's world, instructional assistants are more likely to be instructing students, helping to get group sizes low enough in the small-group interventions. These assistants, who are sometimes called "paraprofessionals" because they may not have teaching credentials, are a critical part of MTSS tiered instruction. They rotate throughout the day, teaching small groups of students alongside classroom teachers.

Providing high-quality professional development for these instructional assistants makes all the difference. Schools getting the greatest gains from their MTSS implementation are providing the assistants with scripted lessons and all the materials they need for a successful lesson. Most assistants are not comfortable creating lessons on their own, and they typically aren't paid to do this.

Consider training the assistants separately from teachers if the district is large enough to have a dozen or more assistants. Many times, assistants don't want to ask a question with classroom teachers in the room. They need to be in an environment that supports their learning.

Just because most assistants aren't certified teachers doesn't mean that the small-group instruction they deliver to students is subpar. Generally, quite the opposite is true. While observing intervention groups in schools, my takeaway is that the instructional assistants are often following the lesson more precisely than the teachers. They tend to focus only on these lessons, whereas teachers are teaching so many different things that intervention can get short-changed. The instructional assistants working in schools across the United States are often real gems, and their work can make or break the level of improvement in the student's reading scores.

Formats for Professional Development

As we know, professional development occurs in various formats. Schools use workshops, coaching sessions, and online training.

Workshops

Workshops are a great venue when the same information needs to be provided to a lot of people; it's more cost-effective to do it once, with everyone in the room at the same time. Workshops also are a good choice when one of the goals is to develop a common language and shared vision. At the outset of implementing MTSS, it's simply more efficient to cover initial information in a workshop setting that can accommodate up to 50 participants. As noted earlier, some of the topics that can be covered in a large group include an overview of the MTSS framework and how to administer and score assessments.

These introductory workshops can be provided separately for each grade level or to clusters of grade levels. Because both the universal screener and the diagnostic assessments for MTSS vary by grade level, the ideal approach is to offer a one-day workshop for teachers at a single grade level across all the schools in a district. If a particular grade level has very few teachers, then groups can be created for K–1, grades 2–3, and grades 4–6.

Coaching Sessions

After teachers attend a one-day introductory workshop, the next step is to provide them with site-based modeling and coaching on instruction. All the classroom teachers at a grade level, plus reading specialists and others who work with struggling readers at that grade level, can meet for a half-day session. The session can begin with a dialogue about how the assessments, grouping, and regrouping are going, with participants having an opportunity to ask questions and learn from one another. After the data discussion, a master teacher or outside consultant can model a lesson with a small group of students while the participants observe. Once the students leave the room, the consultant or master teacher can debrief with the group to discuss what went well, where students struggled, and ways the lesson could have been improved. After watching, it's the teachers' turn. They can each work with one student on a different lesson while the master teacher or consultant circulates to offer feedback and suggestions and to answer questions.

Online Professional Development and Support

Face-to-face professional development is expensive, not only because of the fee and travel expenses of an outside consultant or facilitator, but also because of the cost of substitute teachers. Online alternatives hold promise as a way to effectively provide some types of training—depending on the topic and goal—at less cost.

Online PD can fulfill a couple of purposes. Outside consultants can provide support to teachers between onsite coaching visits. Online PD can also be used to build background knowledge of the teaching staff. Teachers appreciate learning about research and evidence-based practices when this information is integrated with practical training on instructional procedures. One thing that engages teachers is watching videos of teachers instructing students and then reflecting with their colleagues about what they observed.

The online format can help superintendents and other administrators address certain challenges related to teacher professional development. For example, many districts limit the number of days that teachers can be pulled out of the classroom. They face increased sensitivity about losing valuable instructional time and ensuring that substitutes make productive use of their time in the classroom. Availability of substitute teachers is an issue in some districts. It's also challenging to expect an entire grade level of teachers to benefit when one person is sent to a workshop and the others haven't had the same opportunity.

There have been a number of experiments in online training. Free online courses are available worldwide on platforms such as edX and Coursera. The main issue they have faced is low completion rates—sometimes as dismal as 10 percent. Many education companies experimenting with online courses have gotten high completion rates when teachers are offered incentives, such as collecting points toward an increase in base salary or graduate course credits. Offering micro-credentials such as digital badges is a recent approach that enables participants to display their completed courses on their résumés and LinkedIn profiles.

Professional Development Versus Training: The Challenges of Achieving Sustainability

Forward-thinking schools or districts realize that successful implementation and sustainability of MTSS are directly related to the professional development provided, especially in the initial stages. Too often schools implement initiatives without a plan for professional development. Regardless of what the focus of the school reform is, the success of the initiative is highly correlated with the professional development plan.

> Too often schools implement initiatives without a plan for professional development.

Professional development is expensive if done right, and it's important to understand how it differs from training, which is typically more like guided directions on how to use a specific product, or on a skill like how to administer and score an assessment. Professional development, by contrast, typically covers broader foundational knowledge and information about essential processes related to MTSS. Professional development for MTSS should focus on more than training on how to teach a new program or use a particular product. Much of the time should be dedicated to placing the product or lessons within a framework. Topics covered should include a progression of skills displayed on a continuum, types of assessments, research about why MTSS works, and a framework for all the processes and structures of MTSS.

When schools launch MTSS, it's easy for them to think about spending their entire budget on products. However, it's possible that all the funds used to buy products will be a waste without the proper training, which, again, is part of the broader professional development effort. Here's the key question to ask: How many products are sitting on shelves unused? While having the right instructional materials for intervention is critical, the success of those materials is tied directly to professional development that includes modeling of the key instructional routines and coaching for teachers. During product training, it can be helpful for participants to get the instruction via videos. However, participants will also benefit from hands-on time with materials and time to practice a few key lessons or strategies.

Here's one final thought on the topic of professional development and training: establishing a process for how new hires will be brought up to speed is critical for the sustainability phase of MTSS.

Summing Up

Professional development is a key success factor for an effective MTSS implementation. MTSS requires a common language and vision, and groups of educators need to come together to achieve that. The best practice is to plan professional development that is differentiated by role so that administrators, reading coaches, instructional assistants, and teachers are participating in PD that is designed to meet their unique needs. Larger districts may also consider offering sessions for instructional assistants separately from teachers because of their key role in delivering intervention instruction. Professional development can be provided in different formats, including workshops, coaching sessions, and online. Each has different strengths, and the best PD plans will use all three formats but in different ways. Achieving sustainability in MTSS is a challenge, and ensuring comprehensive professional development—which will likely include targeted training for specific materials and products—is essential.

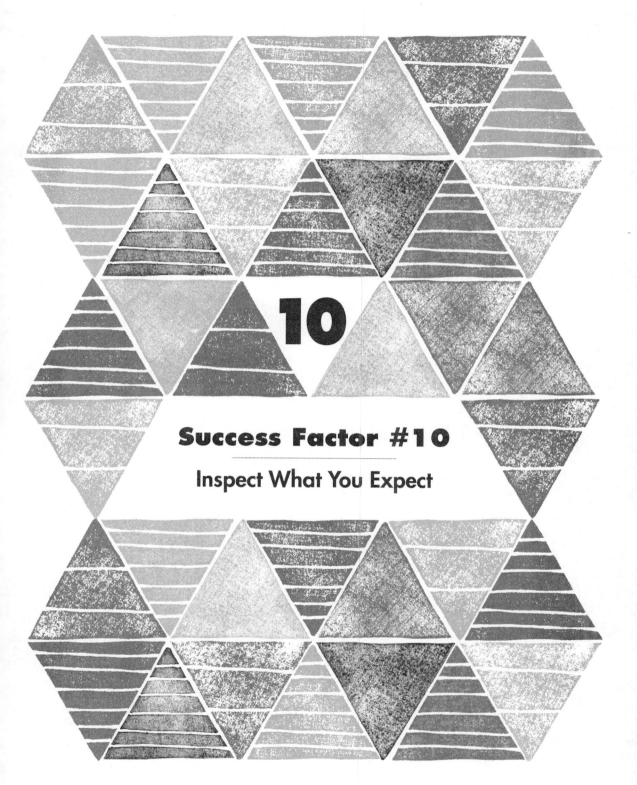

10

Success Factor #10

Inspect What You Expect

Implementing MTSS or RTI in literacy requires a school to put in place many new structures and processes. Teachers learn to use assessment data, including data from diagnostic assessments, in ways that may be completely unfamiliar to them. Progress-monitoring data are key for decision making. The hope is that, with all the meaningful data collected as part of the MTSS process, teachers will experience the satisfaction of no longer having to guess *why* a student is struggling. They can feel empowered to pinpoint exactly what is holding back each student; they can see clearly which students need instruction in the same skills and therefore should be placed together in a group. Teachers report that, before MTSS, they sat in front of intervention groups with some kids nailing each question and others sitting with a blank stare. It was painfully obvious that the needs of the students in the group were not similar enough, and no matter which skill they focused on, it was too easy for some students, too hard for others, and just right for perhaps only one student.

> Teachers report that, before MTSS, they sat in front of intervention groups with some kids nailing each question and others sitting with a blank stare.

With the approach presented in this book, teachers carefully analyze each struggling reader to pinpoint the next skill that particular student needs to close the gaps. Teachers place students in skill groups across a grade level (called Walk-to-Intervention), and extra staff members are scheduled to help, flooding a grade level so that the group sizes are small enough to enable the valuable feedback loop that makes Tier 2 and Tier 3 time so different from time spent on Tier 1. Teachers are provided intervention lessons that not only incorporate research-based instructional practices but also are aligned with the group's focus skill. They participate in effective professional development where they learn about the characteristics of effective intervention instruction. They have the opportunity to watch experts modeling lessons with students so they can see what a well-taught lesson looks like. When first learning the instructional routines, teachers are mentored by an instructional coach or outside reading consultant.

Now it's time to make sure that it all comes together so that students can get the best possible instruction within the tiers of MTSS. All the things described in this chapter introduction are Success Factors 1 through 9. It wouldn't make sense to invest in all the preceding factors and not monitor the outcomes. Thus, Success Factor 10 is about administrators inspecting what they expect.

The phrase "inspect what you expect" may have negative connotations to some people. It can be interpreted as uncomfortably evaluative. That's not the view intended in this book. The types of observations visualized here are designed to provide feedback that is welcome and informative.

Why Observations Matter

Over the past decade, the role of school leadership has moved into the spotlight of education. A Wallace Foundation paper says, "Leadership is second only to classroom instruction as an influence on student learning" (2013, p. 5). This excellent paper discusses the role of the principal as a leader in guiding schools to better teaching and learning, including the importance of observations. It quotes a study by researchers from the University of Minnesota and the University of Toronto that examined the behaviors of principals who were viewed to be high performing and low performing. Among the findings was this:

> High-scoring principals frequently observed classroom instruction for short periods of time, making 20 to 60 observations a week, and most of the observations were spontaneous. Their visits enabled them to make formative observations that were clearly about learning and professional growth, coupled with direct and immediate feedback. High-scoring principals believed that every teacher, whether a first-year teacher or a veteran, can learn and grow. (Wallace Foundation, 2013, p. 14)

The quote includes a key word: *spontaneous*. The type of observations referred to are not the planned evaluative observations that occur at a designated time when the principal sits in a teacher's classroom to watch as much as 90 minutes of classroom instruction. The teacher knows about this observation in advance and often selects the day based on the lesson she wants the principal to observe. This type of observation is part of the school's teacher evaluation system.

The brief observations described in the Wallace Foundation quote must be spontaneous. The teacher can't know that the principal is coming into her classroom because the whole point is for the principal to see what is happening every day, as a normal course of business. Spontaneity matters for this type of observation.

> The teacher can't know that the principal is coming into her classroom because the whole point is for the principal to see what is happening every day, as a normal course of business.

To make 20 to 60 classroom observations a week, principals must be organized. One principal of a large Florida elementary school with 10 sections per grade level had an effective approach. She kept a small laminated card in her pocket with the times when intervention was scheduled for each grade level. Whenever she walked across the building for some other reason, she intentionally diverted her path on the way back to the office so she was passing through the wing where intervention was taking place at that time. She stepped into at least one classroom and watched for 10 minutes or less. The fact that the principal stopped by during intervention time signaled her view that this instructional time mattered—that it shouldn't be a time when any teacher believed it was OK to skate by without advance preparation of group lessons.

Even after making the time to observe, principals may be challenged by how to provide feedback. The Florida principal used a half-page "Intervention Snapshot" form to jot down a few notes of what she saw, and once she got back to the office, she slipped a copy in the teacher's mailbox. The lesson here is this: providing direct and immediate feedback is critical for the process of observation to have the greatest impact.

Conducting Snapshot Observations

Establishing the process for conducting nonevaluative observations requires open communication between the administrator and the teachers. It's important for the administrator to set the tone and make sure that teachers know what to expect when the principal comes in the room.

Over my career, with hundreds of opportunities to walk through an elementary school with a principal, it's pretty clear whether a principal's presence in classrooms is a common occurrence or a novel event. The students are the indicator. If the principal walks in and everything stops and the students turn around to look at the principal, it's likely that an administrator visit is not a common thing. On the other hand, if nothing stops or changes when the principal walks into the classroom, then it's clear that the principal's presence is something that happens frequently—perhaps every couple of days.

The Observation Process

As implied at the start of this chapter, a critical ground rule for the observation process is that it not be evaluative. The process should not be viewed by the staff as part of a teacher's formal evaluation. In addition to the principal conducting short snapshot interventions, it's beneficial to create a culture where peers can observe one another. Reading coaches should be welcome in classrooms—and so should other teachers.

An Observation Form

The form used for brief snapshot observations of intervention instruction should be short and simple. It's better to focus on just a few key areas than to overwhelm the teacher with too much information. In 2009, while consulting in a Florida district, 95 Percent Group Inc. developed a Snapshot Observation Form for training principals in how to observe a 10- to 15-minute period of a Tier 2 or Tier 3 intervention group lesson (see Figure 10.1). The form covers a limited number of items, thus providing a focus.

On the left side of the form, the observer notes where the instruction is taking place, the group size, and whether the lesson focus is obvious and the teacher is referencing the intervention plan and word list. The form highlights eight characteristics, listed in order of importance. Here is what the observer should be looking for, for each characteristic:

FIGURE 10.1
Form for an Intervention Snapshot Observation

95% GROUP INC. **Intervention Snapshot** Teacher: _____ Grade: _____ Date: _____ Time: _____ ☐ Instructional focus: _____ ☐ Group seated at table _____ ☐ # of students in group: _____ (3-5 is ideal) ☐ Intervention plan and word list accessible **Observed evidence of:** ☐ Effective intervention instruction 　☐ Explicit (specific and direct) 　☐ Systematic (consistent) 　☐ Sequential (simple to complex) ☐ Effective modeling 　☐ I do　☐ We do　☐ You do ☐ Pacing and student engagement level ☐ Sufficient corrective feedback ☐ Scaffolding ☐ Differentiation within the group	Comments: _____ Observed by: _____

1. **Effective intervention instruction—Explicit.** Is instruction explicit, with the teacher telling the students exactly what to do? There should be no guessing.

2. **Effective intervention instruction—Systematic.** Are skills taught using a system or a routine? The students should be able to anticipate that a routine will be followed throughout the instructional sequence.

3. **Effective intervention instruction—Sequential.** Are skills taught in a sequence or progression from easiest to hardest?

4. **Effective modeling.** Is there evidence of an "I Do, We Do, You Do" instructional model? This enables a gradual release from teacher to students, with the students first seeing the teacher do an example, then the

teacher and students doing a second example, and finally the students doing one alone while the teacher observes.

5. **Pacing and student engagement level.** Do the students seem engaged in the lesson? Is the teacher's pacing just right for the students?

6. **Sufficient corrective feedback.** Is the teacher giving sufficient corrective feedback? Such feedback is one of the most important benefits of the small-group format of intervention instruction.

7. **Scaffolding.** When a student makes an error, does the teacher provide scaffolding in the form of breaking the task down into smaller steps, or adding manipulatives, or using another means to support the child's learning?

8. **Differentiation within the group.** Does the teacher give students different tasks that vary by what they need? For example, giving some students easier words than others on the "You Do" portion of the lesson would be evidence of differentiation.

These eight characteristics are purposely listed in a specific order. The first four must be in place before the next four can be mastered. First, the instruction must be explicit, systematic, and sequential, and it must include effective modeling. If those four attributes are present, then it's possible for the teacher to refine the art of instruction by paying attention to student engagement and pacing, providing feedback and scaffolding, and differentiating for each student in the group.

The completed form in Figure 10.2 shows that the principal observed 15 minutes of a consonant-vowel-consonant lesson on the short-*a* vowel. A group of four students were seated at a table and the teacher, Ms. Smith, had the lesson plan available for referencing during the lesson. The principal noted evidence of explicit instruction during this lesson. She also made some good notes on students who had particular difficulties, including a focus on Juan. Following the observation, she will spend a few moments asking Ms. Smith about Juan and whether this struggle is typical or he was just having a bad day. The principal wrote down three coaching points at the bottom of the form. She noted that the modeling cycle needs to be more complete; Ms. Smith spent too little time on the "We Do" portion before moving to the "You Do." The lesson would be strengthened by Ms. Smith paying special attention to correcting all student errors and referring to the word list. Even though the pacing of

FIGURE 10.2

Example #1 of a Completed Observation Form

95% GROUP INC. **Intervention Snapshot**	Comments: _9:00–9:03–review–PA (Substitution)_
	PA Review–thumbs up and down for words w/ short a.
Teacher: _Ms. Smith_ Grade: _2_	_Juan had trouble–was watching neighbor_
Date: _Nov. 14_ Time: _9:00–9:15_	
	9:03–9:12–taught concept
☑ Instructional focus: _CVC–short a_	_Word card drill–pointed to a followed by consonant_
☑ Group seated at table _Yes_	_Told student to look for vowel and letter after_
☑ # of students in group: _4_ (3–5 is ideal)	
☑ Intervention plan and word list accessible	_9:12–9:15–reading short-a words_
	I DO–she read words from cards–tap, pat, map
Observed evidence of:	_We DO–only did one word together_
☑ Effective intervention instruction	
☐ Explicit (specific and direct)	_You DO–students read from own card decks (Juan had_
☐ Systematic (consistent)	_trouble–little correction)_
☐ Sequential (simple to complex)	
☐ Effective modeling	
☑ I do ☐ We do ☑ You do	_Excellent systematic instruction_
☐ Pacing and student engagement level	_"say it, repeat it, finger-spell it, read it"_
☐ Sufficient corrective feedback	_I DO was always strong–skipped WE DO often_
☐ Scaffolding	_Pacing slow at times_
☐ Differentiation within the group	
	Suggestions: Increase pacing
	Use word list more
	Correct all student errors
	Observed by: _Principal_

the lesson was a little too slow, expanding the "We Do" and providing more consistent corrective feedback are the first things Ms. Smith needs to focus on before addressing pacing.

On November 14, the principal completed a 15-minute observation on the phonological awareness skill focused on isolating initial sounds in words (see Figure 10.3). There is no note about the number of students in the group, whether they were seated at a table, or whether an intervention lesson plan was visible. On the form it's possible to see that the review portion of the lesson

FIGURE 10.3
Example #2 of a Completed Observation Form

95% GROUP INC. **Intervention Snapshot**
 	
Teacher: _Ms. Riggs_   Grade: _K_
 	
Date: _Nov. 14_   Time: _11:00–11:15_
 	
☑ Instructional focus: _PA–initial sound_
☐ Group seated at table _____
☐ # of students in group: _____ (3-5 is ideal)
☐ Intervention plan and word list accessible
 	
Observed evidence of:
☐ Effective intervention instruction
  ☐ Explicit (specific and direct)
  ☑ Systematic (consistent)
  ☑ Sequential (simple to complex)
☐ Effective modeling
  ☐ I do ☐ We do ☐ You do
☐ Pacing and student engagement level
☐ Sufficient corrective feedback
☐ Scaffolding
☐ Differentiation within the group
	Comments: _11:00–11:15–Review–short-e words_
	Passed out elephants on a stick.
	Students held up elephants when heard short-e words.
	Students responded to 12-15 words in 4 mins–not enough.
	  • _Need to have students close eyes._
	  • _Should have sticks ready–wasted time._
	
	11:05–11:15–Students read CVC words on papers.
	Teacher showed how to blend words–ham, let, hit.
	Then students practiced reading words–sun, bit, set, pot.
	  • _Students confused–concentrate on 1 vowel._
	
	Needs to tell students what to do–model it!
	Do more modeling–didn't see a WE DO.
	
	Suggestions: Wasted time getting manipulatives.
	Students shouldn't be working with print for PA.
	Didn't give students enough feedback and correction.
	Use techniques that prohibit students copying neighbor.
	Observed by: _Principal_

took five minutes, although the lesson plan specified two minutes. In four minutes, the students responded to approximately 12 to 15 words, which are not enough responses for that period of time. They should have responded to at least twice that many. The principal included a suggestion for the teacher, Ms. Riggs, noting that students wouldn't be able to "hitchhike" peers if they closed their eyes during this section of the lesson. During the next section, the principal noted that the students seemed confused by mixing words with different vowels; the examples show that the words contained all five vowel sounds. The principal needs to coach Ms. Riggs to have her materials ready ahead of the lesson, to not use print materials for phonological awareness lessons, to improve her modeling, and to give students more feedback and correction.

Summing Up

The final success factor for implementing MTSS emphasizes the importance of administrators' use of spontaneous short observations to "inspect what you expect" and to provide feedback and coaching for teachers on how to improve their small-group intervention instruction. The use of this practice is validated by research conducted by the University of Minnesota and the University of Toronto that shows that the most effective principals conduct 20 to 60 unscheduled short observations a week. A snapshot intervention form is a useful tool for principals conducting such observations. The form includes "look-for" elements listed in order of importance, and space for notes to share as feedback to the teacher. Although a principal's day is always busy, making time to observe and provide feedback to teachers has to be a priority for schools seeking to achieve impressive results with their MTSS implementation.

Epilogue

I wrote this book because I don't want MTSS to be forgotten like so many other education initiatives. We in the education field too often fall prey to "shiny penny syndrome," wholeheartedly embracing the next new thing while losing momentum on the worthwhile things we've already got. It's not that we consciously believe any new idea is automatically better than the old way of working; rather, our energy and focus simply shift to whatever feels novel and fresh, leaving existing efforts to wither. We have only a limited amount of time and energy; inevitably, when something new becomes the focus, something else dies off.

But MTSS isn't a fad or a shiny penny; it's just good school practice. At the heart of MTSS is a set of processes and practices that help educators use data to inform decisions, thereby ensuring that all students achieve to their maximum potential. Yet the way things are going, it appears that MTSS may lose out to the newest fads. Without proven gains, it will fade away. Numerous schools and districts can say that they tried MTSS and didn't see significant improvements. What these schools don't realize is that their attempt at implementation likely failed because they left out too many components that are essential for success.

In this book, I outline the 10 success factors observable in schools that are getting results with MTSS. This is not a random list; it was reworked over the course of several years of asking myself exactly what the schools garnering significant gains in student literacy measures were doing differently from those with lackluster results. The 10 factors I eventually arrived at are the distillation of years of observation, fieldwork, and reflection.

These success factors are the defining elements that enable significant gains to happen. They are the processes missing in the schools that believe they are implementing MTSS yet are not achieving improvements in student literacy scores.

Any school can implement these 10 success factors. The evidence is overwhelming that they are effective. Yet waiting for evidence is not the important part; determination, vision, and persistence to stay the course are what matter most. This is not an overnight endeavor. It takes three to five years for a school to fully implement MTSS. Although that will require a commitment, it's well worth it.

References

California Department of Education. (n.d.). *Comparing MTSS to RtI²*. California Department of Education website. Retrieved from http://www.cde.ca.gov/ci/cr/ri/mtsscomprti2.asp

Finnigan, K., & Daly, A. (2017). The trust gap: Understanding the effects of leadership churn in school districts. *American Educator, 41*(2), 24–29.

Gillon, G. (2004). *Phonological awareness: From research to practice*. New York: Guilford Press.

Hall, S. L. (2006). *I've DIBEL'd, now what?* Frederick, CO: Sopris West.

Kilpatrick, D. (2015). *Essentials of assessing, preventing, and overcoming reading difficulties*. Hoboken, NJ: Wiley.

Mas, C. (2016). MTSS—The unfulfilled promise. Seattle Schools Community Forum [blog]. Retrieved from http://saveseattleschools.blogspot.com/search?q=MTSS+-+The+Unfulfilled+Promise

National Reading Panel. (2000). *Teaching children to read: An evidence-based assessment of the scientific research literature on reading and its implications for reading instruction*. Washington, DC: National Institutes of Health, National Institute of Child Health and Human Development.

Wallace Foundation. (2013). *The school principal as leader: Guiding schools to better teaching and learning*. Wallace Perspectives Series. Retrieved from Wallace Foundation at http://www.wallacefoundation.org/knowledge-center/Documents/The-School-Principal-as-Leader-Guiding-Schools-to-Better-Teaching-and-Learning-2nd-Ed.pdf

Index

Note: Page references followed by an italicized *f* indicate information contained in figures.

About the Author

Susan L. Hall, EdD, is cofounder and CEO of 95 Percent Group Inc., an educational company whose mission is to help teachers and administrators identify and address the needs of struggling readers. 95 Percent Group provides professional development, diagnostic assessments, and instructional materials to teachers so that they have the knowledge base and tools to improve outcomes for struggling readers. Dr. Hall is especially known for her expertise on the use of literacy assessment data to inform differentiated instruction delivered in small groups to address specific skill deficits. For over 10 years, she served as a national LETRS trainer, and she is a DMG DIBELS Mentor Trainer. She also serves on the Dean's Leadership Council at the Harvard Graduate School of Education. Dr. Hall is the author or coauthor of seven books about reading development, including *I've DIBEL'd, Now What? Next Edition* (Sopris, 2012), *Jumpstart RTI* (Corwin, 2011), and *Implementing Response to Intervention* (Corwin, 2008). She can be reached at shall@95percentgroup.com.

Related ASCD Resources

At the time of publication, the following resources were available (ASCD stock numbers appear in parentheses).

PD Online® Courses

Literacy Strategies: Phonemic Awareness and Vocabulary Building (#PD09OC50M)

Six Research-Based Literacy Approaches for the Elementary Classroom (#PD09OC24M)

Print Products

A Close Look at Close Reading: Teaching Students to Analyze Complex Texts, Grades K–5 by Diane Lapp, Barbara Moss, Maria Grant, and Kelly Johnson (#114008)

Achieving Next Generation Literacy: Using the Tests (You Think) You Hate to Help the Students You Love by Maureen Connolly and Vicky Giouroukakis (#116023)

Differentiated Literacy Coaching: Scaffolding for Student and Teacher Success by Mary Catherine Moran (#107053)

Literacy Unleashed: Fostering Excellent Reading Instruction Through Classroom Visits by Bonnie D. Houck and Sandi Novak (#116042)

Read, Write, Lead: Breakthrough Strategies for Schoolwide Literacy Success by Regie Routman (#113016)

Reading, Writing, and Rigor: Helping Students Achieve Greater Depth of Knowledge in Literacy by Nancy Boyles (#118026)

Total Literacy Techniques: Tools to Help Students Analyze Literature and Informational Texts by Pérsida Himmele, William Himmele, and Keely Potter (#114009)

For up-to-date information about ASCD resources, go to www.ascd.org. You can search the complete archives of *Educational Leadership* at www.ascd.org/el.

ASCD myTeachSource®

Download resources from a professional learning platform with hundreds of research-based best practices and tools for your classroom at http://myteachsource.ascd.org/.

For more information, send an e-mail to member@ascd.org; call 1-800-933-2723 or 703-578-9600; send a fax to 703-575-5400; or write to Information Services, ASCD, 1703 N. Beauregard St., Alexandria, VA 22311-1714 USA.

THE WHOLE CHILD

The ASCD Whole Child approach is an effort to transition from a focus on narrowly defined academic achievement to one that promotes the long-term development and success of all children. Through this approach, ASCD supports educators, families, community members, and policymakers as they move from a vision about educating the whole child to sustainable, collaborative actions.

10 Success Factors for Literacy Intervention relates to the **supported** tenet. *For more about the ASCD Whole Child approach, visit* **www.ascd.org/wholechild.**

WHOLE CHILD
TENETS

1 HEALTHY
Each student enters school healthy and learns about and practices a healthy lifestyle.

2 SAFE
Each student learns in an environment that is physically and emotionally **safe** for students and adults.

3 ENGAGED
Each student is actively engaged in learning and is connected to the school and broader community.

4 SUPPORTED
Each student has access to personalized learning and is supported by qualified, caring adults.

5 CHALLENGED
Each student is challenged academically and prepared for success in college or further study and for employment and participation in a global environment.